"Dr. Maher has produced one of the most excellent texts I've read in my past 30 years related to the systems-based approach of creating a proactive model of mental health care for athletes, coaches, and organizations. His experience, knowledge, and 'real world' applications form a solid foundation for this book that will be a 'must read' reference for psychologists, mental health providers, sports medicine staff, coaches, and athletics administrators. The recent movement in mental health care for athletes in all levels of sport requires a book such as this to help guide and direct future programs from a professional and competency-based approach. As a practicing counseling sport psychologist, I've valued Dr. Maher's expertise, knowledge, and collegiality for the past 20+ years...this book is an essential and necessary resource in further developing professional mental health care in the arena of sports at all levels."

Chris Carr, *Director of Performance Psychology, Green Bay Packers, USA*

"In *Fostering the Mental Health of Athletes, Coaches, and Staff*, Dr. Charlie Maher uses a practical systems approach and draws on his 30+ years of experience fostering mental and emotional health of athletes and coaches in professional and collegiate sports to explain how to develop a psychologically healthy organization for competitive excellence. A must read!"

Elizabeth L. Shoenfelt, *Professor Emerita of Psychology at Western Kentucky University, USA*

"This is an excellent and accessible introduction for practitioners interested in using a systems approach to foster the mental health of athletes, coaches, and staff in sport organizations. In each chapter, Dr Maher covers a range of mental health-enhancing possibilities and offers wonderful insight to how these might be realised. This book is exactly what is needed within the field at this moment; After reading it you will come to appreciate that promoting mental health in sport is a multi-level task in nature and scope and requires attention, programs, and services at individual, team, and organizational levels."

Dr Chris Wagstaff, *Reader in Applied Psychology, University of Portsmouth, UK*

T0383542

Fostering the Mental Health of Athletes, Coaches, and Staff

This book describes a systems approach for fostering the mental health of athletes, coaches, and staff in sport organizations at professional, collegiate, and secondary school levels. Through this approach, readers can collaborate effectively with a range of professionals in sport organizations, helping to create a mentally healthy entity.

Fostering the Mental Health of Athletes, Coaches, and Staff includes a set of sequential, interrelated chapters that detail precise steps along with practitioner exercises. Following an introductory chapter about the evolution of mental health in sport organizations, the systems approach is overviewed in terms of its constituent dimensions. Chapter-by-chapter guidance then is provided about the following activities:

- Creating a vision and direction for mental health in a sport organization.
- Assessing the readiness of a sport organization for mental health initiatives.
- Identifying and involving people as key contributors to mental health.
- Assessing the mental and emotional development of athletes, coaches, and staff.
- Designing and implementing mental health programs and services.
- Educating and training coaches, staff, and administrators about mental health.
- Establishing a team environment conducive to mental health.
- Formulating and enacting mental health policies, plans, and procedures.
- Coordinating mental skills, life skills, and mental health.
- Evaluating mental health programs and services.
- Making decisions about improving mental health initiatives.

Through its unique and important nature and scope, as well as being the first of its kind to discuss athlete mental health through this specific lens, this book is essential for licensed sport, clinical, and counseling psychologists, as well as other professionals who communicate and collaborate regarding mental health, including mental performance consultants, athletic trainers, and administrators.

Charles A. Maher, PsyD, CMPC, FAASP is a licensed psychologist, sport and performance psychologist with the Cleveland Guardians Baseball Organization, and Professor Emeritus of Applied Psychology at Rutgers University, New Jersey, USA. For thirty-four years, Dr Maher has provided mental performance and mental health services to athletes, coaches, support staffs, and executives in Major League Baseball, National Basketball Association, Women's National Basketball Association, National Football League, National Hockey League, collegiate sport organizations, as well as in tennis, boxing, and horseracing.

CHARLES A. MAHER

Fostering the Mental Health of Athletes, Coaches, and Staff

A Systems Approach to Developing a Mentally Healthy Sport Organization

NEW YORK AND LONDON

Cover image: Getty Images

First published 2023
by Routledge
605 Third Avenue, New York, NY 10158

and by Routledge
4 Park Square, Milton Park, Abingdon, Oxon, OX14 4RN

Routledge is an imprint of the Taylor & Francis Group, an informa business

Library of Congress Cataloging-in-Publication Data
Names: Maher, Charles A., 1944- author.
Title: Fostering the mental health of athletes, coaches, and staff : a systems approach to developing a mentally healthy sport organization / Charles A. Maher.
Description: New York, NY : Routledge, 2022. | Includes bibliographical references and index. | Identifiers: LCCN 2022007056 (print) | LCCN 2022007057 (ebook) | ISBN 9780367746766 (hardback) | ISBN 9780367746742 (paperback) | ISBN 9781003159018 (ebook)
Subjects: LCSH: Sports--Psychological aspects. | Athletes--Mental health. | Coaches (Athletics)--Mental health. | Sports personnel--Mental health.
Classification: LCC GV706.4 .M326 2022 (print) | LCC GV706.4 (ebook) | DDC 796.01/9--dc23/eng/20220604
LC record available at https://lccn.loc.gov/2022007056
LC ebook record available at https://lccn.loc.gov/2022007057

ISBN: 978-0-367-74676-6 (hbk)
ISBN: 978-0-367-74674-2 (pbk)
ISBN: 978-1-003-15901-8 (ebk)

DOI: 10.4324/9781003159018

Typeset in Joanna MT
by KnowledgeWorks Global Ltd.

Contents

The mental health of athletes is a rapidly developing area of research and practice in sport psychology and related disciplines. This emergence of a focus on mental health exists at collegiate, professional, and elite levels, as well as secondary school settings. As a licensed psychologist and sport and performance psychologist in sport organizations, I have been involved in the field of mental health in sport organizations for over 33 years.

Early in my professional practice, I was not explicitly using the term "mental health" when working with athletes, coaches, and staff in sport organizations. However, I have always sought to make sure that my work focused on the total individual—their mental and emotional development—as a performer and person, within the context of a sport organization. I continue to value this kind of whole-person orientation and apply this perspective in my own work and practice.

Over the years, I have tried my best to design and implement programs, services, and systems to support and enhance the mental and emotional development of athletes, coaches, and staff as performers and people. In so doing, I have relied on the use of a systems approach as an overarching framework in my professional practice regarding mental performance and mental health.

Furthermore, I have learned much about the relationship between mental health and the development and performance of athletes. Based on a systems approach, I have realized now more than ever the importance of considering mental health in sport organizations broadly, as encompassing many levels (individual, team, and organization) and involving a range of stakeholders (athletes, coaches, support staffs, and executives).

Without a doubt, many individuals associated with a range of professional disciplines and lines of work are concerned with the mental health of athletes. These professionals include sport psychologists, mental performance consultants, athletic trainers, team physicians, strength and conditioning staffs, athletic coaches, directors of athletics, and front office executives. Relatedly, athletes and those people who provide athletes with social support, including parents and spouses, have expressed interest and concern about mental health and the availability and value of mental health programs and services.

To date, there is a growing body of research, opinions, and anecdotes related to athlete mental health and mental health in sport settings. Much of the published information has focused on the individual athlete and the treatment of mental health disorders, guided essentially by a medical model. However, growing attention has been given to the importance of considering mental health at team and organizational levels. Still, what is less apparent is research or writing concerning the development of perspectives, practices, and procedures that emphasize how to leverage the interconnectedness of individual, team, and organizational levels of intervention in support of mental health in a sport organization.

This challenge of fostering the mental health of athletes is an important sport organizational task. The task also can be broadened to addressing the mental health needs of coaches and other staff. Moreover, when viewed from a systems approach perspective, the task can lead to the development of a mentally healthy sport organization. This is possible not only for a professional sport franchise, but also for a division of intercollegiate athletics, a secondary school athletic department, or even a youth sports program.

All of these reasons led to my decision to author this book. My intention is to provide perspectives and practical guidelines for fostering the mental health of athletes, coaches, and other stakeholders in sport organizations. These organizations include collegiate, professional, and secondary school organizations as well as other entities in which athletes are engaged in competitive sport.

When I thought about mental health in sport and about authoring a book on that topic, several questions came to mind. These questions are ones that I have dealt with and that have influenced me throughout my professional practice in sport organizations. I considered these questions my guide for developing the book.

Subsequently, the following questions helped me to focus the format and content of the book:

1. How can "mental health" in a sport organization be explained so the term has meaning for athletes, coaches, staff, and other stakeholders?
2. What is a practical way the mental health and well-being of athletes can be defined within the context of a sport organization?
3. How can sport organizations promote mental health so that mental health will be an integral part of the organization, rather than being relegated to marginal status?
4. Since coaches, staff, and administrators have influence over the development and performance of athletes, how can their own mental health needs also be addressed?
5. How can a sport organization be structured so it is a mentally healthy one?
6. What kind of overarching framework can be used for the delivery of programs and services related to the mental health of athletes and those who support athletes?
7. What qualifications are necessary for those who provide mental health services in a sport organization?
8. How can a book beneficially provide information so that practitioners of sport psychology can take a meaningful lead in fostering mental health in a sport organization?
9. How can content about mental health in sport organizations be presented in a professional book so the information contained in the chapters of the book adheres to the following criteria?
   - Practicality: Reflects perspectives, guidelines, methods, and procedures that practitioners can use in support of the mental and emotional development, well-being, and performance of athletes, coaches, and staff.
   - Utility: Specifies direction and guidance to the practitioner about how to foster mental health in a sport organization.
   - Propriety: Adheres to the ethical codes of psychology associations as well as to legal entities such as licensing boards.
   - Relevance: Based on defensible evidence from research and professional practice relating to the mental health of athletes, coaches, and staff.

10. How can a systems approach be used as a basis for developing a mentally healthy sport organization?
11. What are indictors of a mentally healthy sport organization?
12. Why does mental health matter to athletes, coaches, and staff?

The information I provide in this book stems from the above questions. The book is intended to be a resource guide for practitioners of sport psychology who desire to assume a leadership role. This leadership role involves helping to guide the development and responsiveness of their sport organizations toward the mental health needs of athletes and others—and to do so in a systematic, multidimensional manner. In this regard, the book seeks to be innovative and state of the art, informed by relevant theory and research as well as being experientially influenced by my own professional practice.

Accordingly, this book offers information about the following:

- The nature and scope of a sport organization, especially concerning both how particular factors, if left unchecked, can put the mental health of athletes at risk and how other factors, if carefully addressed, can serve to protect athletes from mental health problems.
- Parameters of a systems approach and ways its application can meaningfully address the mental health needs of athletes and others at individual, team, and organizational levels.
- Determination of the readiness of a sport organization for encouraging and supporting mental health initiatives.
- Delineation of a practical and positive definition of athlete mental health that is relevant to the sport context.
- Promotion of a culture that commits to fostering mental health in a sport organization.
- Description of a process for the design, implementation, and evaluation of mental health prevention programs as well as programs and services for athletes with mental health concerns, problems, and disorders.
- Enhancement of a team environment that reflects a mental health emphasis and that incorporates the active involvement of athletes, coaches, and support staff.
- Structure of the overall sport organization regarding matters such as coach education about mental health, adherence to ethical

standards and legal codes, diversity and inclusion, mental health action planning, and hiring and supervision of qualified mental health professionals.

NATURE AND SCOPE OF A SYSTEMS APPROACH TO MENTAL HEALTH IN SPORT ORGANIZATIONS

This book presents a systems approach as a broad-based way of addressing the multidimensional task of fostering the mental health of athletes, coaches, support staffs, administrators, and executives in a range of sport organizations. These dimensions include the individual, the team, and the organization.

I have chosen a systems approach as the framework since it has proven valuable to me, professional colleagues, and my graduate students over the years. More basically and most important, a systems approach, as presented in this book, has value for practitioners of sport psychology in the following ways: (a) it allows for an understanding of the interconnectedness of individual, team, and organizational levels; (b) it enables the identification of risk and protective factors that have relevance for athlete mental health; (c) it highlights the importance of involving a range of stakeholders who can contribute to the process of fostering mental health; and (d) it emphasizes the value of building a mentally healthy sport organization.

This book will define a "sport organization" as an entity in which athletes compete that provides professional resources to the athlete and others in support of their development and performance. Given this definition, here are examples of sport organizations:

- Professional sports franchise.
- Division of intercollegiate athletics.
- Elite sport performance academy.
- Olympic or Paralympic sports unit.
- Department of secondary school athletics.

Within the context of a systems approach, athlete "mental health" will be understood in terms of the mental and emotional development of the individual, not as the absence of mental illness. Thus, working from the definition of mental health as defined by the World Health Organization (WHO) in 2013, athlete mental health will be defined as

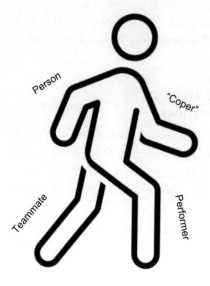

Figure 0.1 Dimensions of Mental Health

a state of well-being where the athlete (or coach or another) manifests the following qualities:

- *Understands* they have personal abilities and skills that are important to their sport and their life over and above how they compete—the athlete as a *person.*
- *Copes* in an effective manner with the demands of their sport and life while seeking positive social and emotional guidance from their support systems—the athlete as a *"coper."*
- *Contributes* in a productive manner to their team and community— the athlete as a *teammate.*
- *Performs* in a manner that leverages preparation, execution, and self-evaluation—the athlete as a *performer.*

Furthermore, a systems approach helps center the task of fostering the mental health of athletes and others at three separate yet interrelated levels:

- The *individual* athlete's mental health.
- The environment of the *team* as a means of supporting mental health.
- The *organization* and its structure for setting the conditions for mental health services delivery.

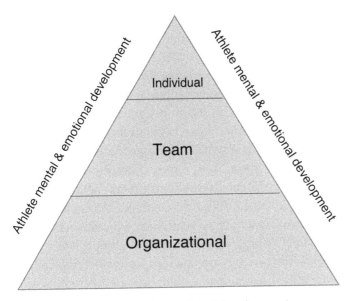

Athlete mental & emotional development

Figure 0.2 Three Levels of Athlete Mental and Emotional Development

FOUNDATIONS OF THE BOOK

The book is based on my 33 years of experience fostering the mental and emotional development of athletes, coaches, and other stakeholders in professional and collegiate sports. Relatedly, and most important, the content of the book is based on conceptions and research in sport and performance psychology and other areas of psychology that pertain to mental health. These experiences and empirical evidence have coalesced to shape my beliefs and premises about mental health in sport organizations. These beliefs and premises are ones I would like to share with you here, since they serve as an entry point for the chapters of the book.

1. "Mental health" in a sport organization is an important subject, one that requires a clear definition of the term. Mental health reflects the mental and emotional well-being of the athletes, coaches, and staff. Within the context of sport organizations, the practitioner pays particular attention to guiding athletes, coaches, and staff to use their thoughts, emotions, and actions in support of themselves as performers and people. Furthermore, mental health is not to be equated with the absence of a mental disorder. Rather,

mental health is a state of positive, productive well-being; it has to do with the domains of mental and emotional development.

2. A "mental health intervention" is a term typically used in psychology and related helping professions. From a systems approach perspective, a mental health intervention is any kind of program, service, or purposeful action that is designed and implemented so that an athlete or other sport organization stakeholder can develop mentally and emotionally and function in positive ways both in and outside sport. Thus, a mental health intervention is not to be equated with mental health treatment; rather, there are various types of mental health interventions. For instance, some interventions are meant to be preventive and educational in nature and are provided as programs to teams and groups, while other mental health interventions are intended for the development of coping and related psychological skills and are offered one-on-one and in group formats. Still other interventions address specific mental health problems and disorders of the individual as individualized programs.

3. Specific mental health problems and disorders relevant to athletes include, but are not limited to, anxiety and related disorders, depression, attention deficit disorder, post-traumatic stress, substance use, sleep problems, and disordered eating.

4. It is useful to portray the mental health of athletes, coaches, and staff as positive and developmental in nature and scope. This positive focus leads the individual to *understand* themself as a performer and person, to *cope* in an effective way with stress and the risks encountered in sport environments, to *relate* in an appropriate way with teammates, and to *perform* in a consistent, quality manner. Relatedly, we nevertheless should make distinctions between subclinical mental health concerns and problems and those mental health disorders that meet established diagnostic criteria such as those found in the Diagnostic and Statistical Manual of Mental Disorders (DSM-5) and International Classification of Disease (ICD) codes.

5. The mental health of athletes is best considered within the range of contexts in which they train, perform, and live. Important specific contexts include rules and expectations unique to their sports, the predominant cultures in which the athletes operate,

and the ethnicities and languages of their country of origin, as well as the athlete's personal identity, their linguistic competence, and their history and level of competition.

6. To experience success within competitive venues, athletes often pay more attention to how they perform and less to who they are as a person. Accordingly, it is the responsibility of those who work with athletes in support of their mental health to help them learn to be cognizant of not only what they do (performer) but also who they are, over and above performance (person).

7. When athletes possess a set of clarified values (guiding principles), they can anchor themselves to be the best version of themselves possible, not only as performers but also as people. In this way, athletes are more likely than not to effectively balance sport with life and manifest mental health. Therefore, the clarification of values and a commitment to values-guided actions are central to athlete mental health.

8. Assessment of the mental health needs of athletes is best considered a dynamic approach. A dynamic assessment approach involves the use of sport-specific perspectives as well as multiple methods and procedures; it includes data being gathered over the course of time and continuously monitoring mental health needs and contexts over time. Such methods and procedures may involve questionnaires, interviews, observations, interactive exercises, and discussions, with due regard for the ethnicity and linguistic competency of the athletes. Relatedly, and most important, only professionals qualified to provide such assessment services should supervise and undertake the assessment of the mental health needs of athletes.

9. Although diagnostic procedures that emphasize a search for psychopathology in discrete diagnostic categories may be necessary for certain athletes, the mental health of athletes should not be limited to these.

10. A systems approach allows those focused on the task of fostering the mental health of athletes to identify and coordinate programs and services at three separate yet interrelated levels: (a) the individual mental health of an athlete, coach, or staff member; (b) the team environment regarding mental health; and (c) the structure of the organization in which athletes, coaches, and staff operate.

11. Given these three levels of mental health intervention—individual, team, and organizational—we can identify risk and protective factors at each level. Risk factors are traditions, norms, and circumstances that make the athlete, team, or sport organization vulnerable to concerns, problems, and disorders related to the mental health of athletes, coaches, and staff. Protective factors serve to mitigate mental health risks and promote positive mental and emotional experiences for all concerned.

12. Through programs and services at individual, team, and organizational levels, including ongoing progress monitoring, a systems approach increases the likelihood of the development and maintenance of a mentally healthy organization.

13. In order to foster the mental health of athletes, coaches, and staff in a sport organization, practitioners must give concerted attention to the education and training of all these stakeholders regarding mental health.

14. Qualified, licensed mental health providers need to be hired and made readily available to athletes and others in sport organizations for education, training, guidance, and treatment.

15. Defensible policies and procedures are necessary and must be in place for the administration and supervision of a mental health program.

16. A comprehensive mental health program is best developed and sustained by means of a systematic process: (a) clarification of mental health needs within the relevant contexts; (b) design of the program, based on assessed needs and context; (c) monitoring of the implementation of the program; and (d) evaluation of the program as a basis for its continued development and improvement.

17. All programs and services and personnel that relate to mental health in sport organizations must conform to ethical codes such as those of the American Psychological Association and the Association for Applied Sport Psychology, coupled with adherence to all relevant legal standards and codes.

FORMAT OF THE CHAPTERS OF THE BOOK

This book has been written for practitioners of sport psychology whose roles make them responsible for ensuring that the mental health needs of athletes, coaches, and staff are addressed through appropriate programs and services. These practitioners may be in the fields of sport and performance psychology, clinical and counseling psychology, and clinical social work, yet the book also applies to executives and other leaders in sport organizations. The book is meant to be a practical guide you can use to foster the mental health of athletes, coaches, and staff in sport organizations at professional, collegiate, and secondary school levels. In turn, such work is likely to lead to developing a mentally healthy sport organization.

Each of the chapters of the book includes the following features:

- Statement of purpose of the chapter and overview of its content.
- Detailed presentation of the chapter material and explanation of why it was developed in that way.
- Selected review and commentary about conceptions and research that relate to the chapter.
- Practitioner guidelines to assist an individual to engage in the tasks discussed in the chapter.
- Case examples to illustrate points made in the chapter.
- End of chapter exercises for the practitioner to use to reflect on the material in the chapter and to see the chapter's relevance for their own work as well as for their continued development and improvement.

Charles A. Maher
Cleveland, Ohio
May 2022

Acknowledgments

There are many people in professional and collegiate sport organizations who, over the years, have contributed to this book in terms of their interest, support, involvement, perspectives, and expertise regarding the mental health and well-being of athletes, coaches, and staff. These people include coaches, mental performance consultants, sport psychologists, athletic trainers, strength and conditioning staff, athletes, athletic administrators, and front office executives. To all these people, I provide my appreciation and gratitude for helping to develop sport organizations that are mentally healthy entities. I also thank my wife, Ann, for her continued understanding and patience with me as I authored this book and engaged in my professional practice. Finally, and very importantly, I extend my heartfelt thanks to Sandy Lynn Haney, my trusted and skilled editorial assistant. Sandy's contributions to this book are manifold and include providing insightful and relevant advice about how to present subject matter, technical guidance, timely feedback, and overall support.

One

This chapter provides an overview of mental health in relation to sport organizations. This overview offers conceptual and operational perspectives that will serve as a foundation for subsequent chapters of the book. Accordingly, mental health in sport organizations will be discussed in ways that have import for practitioners who work with athletes, coaches, and staff in organizational contexts. First, the chapter offers a brief overview of the evolution of mental health in general. Second, it discusses conceptions and definitions of mental health regarding mental health in sports. Third, it gives a definition of mental health for use in sport organizations. Fourth, the chapter considers risk and protective factors that relate to mental health in sport organizations at individual, team, and organizational levels. Fifth, it makes distinctions regarding mental skills, life skills, and mental health. Sixth, it presents the nature, scope, and indicators of a mentally healthy sport organization. Finally, the chapter offers exercises for practitioners.

BRIEF OVERVIEW OF THE EVOLUTION OF MENTAL HEALTH
AS RELATED TO SPORT

The mental health of individuals in the United States and other countries has been an area of concern for researchers and practitioners in psychiatry, psychology, and related professional disciplines for hundreds of years (Keyes, 2013). Over the past 50 years or so, the conception of mental health with respect to general populations has readily transformed; significant changes have been made in the nature and scope of how people view the mental health domain (Keyes, 2002; WHO, 2004). Significant changes include the closure of mental health asylums, the move of mental health care into community venues vis-à-vis community mental health centers (WHO, 2004), the increased use of cognitive behavioral approaches to the treatment of mental health disorders (Breslin & Leavey, 2019), and the development of

DOI: 10.4324/9781003159018-1

methods and procedures for screening and prevention of mental health problems (Galderisi et al., 2015).

One significant change has been a shift in the attitudes of people toward what mental health is and what it means to foster people's mental health. This shift also includes changes of attitudes about mental health in the sports, including at professional and collegiate levels (MacIntrye et al., 2017). Previously, players, coaches, and other sport stakeholders primarily viewed mental health in relation to sports in terms of the mental illness of the individual. The focus thus was on dealing with an individual's mental problems, often in a reactive manner. For instance, when I began my work in professional sports 33 years ago, other athletes and coaches labeled an athlete who was thought to have a mental problem as being unfit to play, not mentally tough, or possessing a mental illness. As a practitioner, I was asked to fix the "mental case" so the athlete could play and perform well, no matter what the cost to the individual. If the athlete did not perform well due to mental health, it was likely they would be released from the team.

More recently, though, viewpoints about mental health in sport have evolved for the better among athletes and others in sport organizational contexts. In this regard, athletes as well as those groups that oversee sports are becoming increasingly aware of the mental health problems of athletes, and they are willing to provide support for athletes with mental health issues. The acceptance of the importance of the mental health of athletes, coupled with the willingness of other stakeholders to support mental health in sport, is reflected in part by an increasing number of high-profile athletes who have taken a stand about the need for mental health services.

Relatedly, professional organizations that oversee sport, such as Major League Baseball, the National Football League, the National Basketball Association, and the National Collegiate Athletic Association, have taken concerted steps to focus on athlete mental health. Even more encouraging has been the desire among athletes, executives, and researchers to consider mental health in a proactive way: they have called for educational programs about mental health and for forward-looking mental health prevention concepts and initiatives that can be implemented in sport organizations (Hong & Rao, 2020; Moesch et al., 2018).

During the past two decades, the World Health Organization (WHO) has been a leading force in framing mental health not just as an absence of mental illness but also as a state encompassing the psychological, social, and emotional well-being of the individual. In addition, theory and research related to mental health have taken a broader view, with several models emphasizing that mental health can be seen on a continuum from mental distress to positive mental health (see, e.g., Keyes, 2002, 2007). In particular, people are becoming more aware of frequently occurring mental health disorders, such as depression and anxiety, and individuals and groups are more willing to seek services from mental health professionals.

Clearly, mental health also has come to the fore in relation to the mental health of collegiate, professional, and other elite athletes. The range of prominent athletes who have become vocal and who have discussed their mental health problems through social media has further emphasized the rise in the importance of athlete mental health. Examples of such athletes include Michael Phelps in swimming, DeMar DeRozan and Kevin Love in basketball, Simone Biles in gymnastics, Naomi Osaka in tennis, Drew Robinson in baseball, and many others.

According to the National Institute of Mental Health, 43.4 million American adults reported having some mental health diagnosis. Furthermore, studies have revealed that between 16 and 20 percent of adults may have had at least one major depressive episode in their lifetime (Kessler et al., 2005; Shim et al., 2011; Walsh, 2011). Mental health concerns among collegiate, professional, and other elite athletes have become increasingly apparent through survey research reports, particularly at the collegiate level, although there has been a call for more systematic studies (Rice et al., 2016). To date, evidence suggests that rates of mental health disorders in athletes could be comparable to rates in the general population and, in some subgroups, possibly higher (Bauman, 2015; Reardon & Factor, 2010; Rice et al., 2019).

As practitioners, it is important for us to understand the history and evolution of mental health in sport. This understanding is particularly important for us since now, more than ever, athletes, coaches, and staff are likely to benefit when mental health is considered integral to the sport enterprise, particularly the sport organization. Furthermore, one aspect of our job as practitioners is to ensure athletes and others have information about the history of mental health both in terms of its evolution and future direction, especially concerning its contribution to athletes as performers and people.

WHO has been an international leader in fostering a positive viewpoint of mental health. One significant contribution it has made is the portrayal of mental health as an asset to the individual and not simply an absence of mental illness. Toward that end, WHO has defined mental health as "a state of well-being in which the individual realizes his or her own abilities, can cope with the normal stresses of life, can work productively and fruitfully, and is able to make a contribution to his or her community" (2013).

Within the above definitional context, there are many external and internal factors that can contribute to an individual athlete's mental and emotional development and well-being (Reardon et al., 2019). These factors touch all aspects of the life of the athlete, within and outside competitive venues. These factors include but are not limited to the following: relationships with coaches and family members; the quality of clubhouse and locker room environments; the diverse makeup of athletes, coaches, and staff; financial matters; and athletes' development of mental skills and life skills. When one or more of these factors become overwhelming or difficult to address, they can affect the mental health of the athlete in ways that are not positive for the athlete (Fletcher & Sarkar, 2012). In turn, the athlete's mental health can affect other relevant stakeholders, such as parents and spouses (Poucher et al., 2021).

The systems approach I describe in the ensuing chapters of the book meshes nicely with WHO's definition of mental health and its recognition of the complexity of mental health. The systems approach has been helpful to me in my work as a sport and performance psychologist for sport organizations. When I started my work in the sport psychology field many years ago, I was intensely focused on the individual athlete and neglected to place the individual and their needs into a larger team and organizational context. As I matured in my own professional development and practice, I came to realize the value of a systems perspective and approach.

The systems approach allows me to recognize and pay due respect to factors that support or limit the mental health of athletes and others at individual, team, and organizational levels. Consequently, using the systems approach as the framework on which this book rests, we will consider mental health in sports in a multi-level way: that is, as positive mental and emotional development and not simply as an absence of mental illness.

A DEFINITION OF MENTAL HEALTH FOR SPORT ORGANIZATIONS

Based on the definition of mental health as promulgated by WHO, I have found it useful for athletes, coaches, and staff to have a clear conception of what is meant by mental health. When people are aware of and understand the definition, it is easier to engage them in mental health initiatives. (Their engagement may involve them being willing to serve as participants in educational and preventive mental health programs and services.) Relatedly, it is easier for them to learn that mental health and mental performance are linked to effective competitiveness. They also can see that the application of mental skills and life skills—areas with which they are more familiar—can promote mental health.

Accordingly, I have created a more comprehensive definition of mental health that is very specific and functional and can be applied to athletes, coaches, and staff. It is based both on my range of professional experiences and on the call from researchers and practitioners for a broad-based conception of mental health (Breslin & Leavey, 2019; Moesch et al., 2018).

The following definition has made sense not only to athletes but also to coaches, staff, and administrators. Within the context of sport organizations and my work with athletes, coaches, and staff, therefore, I have utilized it as a basis for fostering mental health of athletes, coaches, and staff. I encourage you to consider using this definition, too.

"Positive mental health" of an individual in a sport organization is a state of well-being in which the athlete, coach, and/or staff member manifests these mental and emotional qualities:

- *Understands* their values, vision, and personality: the athlete as a *person*, over and above their sport.
- *Copes* in an effective manner with risks they encounter within and outside competitive venues, such as unsavory people, unsafe places, harmful things (e.g., banned substances), and other circumstances (e.g., adversity): the athlete as an effective "*coper*."
- *Interacts* productively with teammates, coaches, staff, the media, fans, and other key people in their lives: the athlete as a *teammate*, given their roles, responsibilities, and relationships within and outside competitive venues.
- *Performs* in a consistent, quality manner through their preparation for competition, their maintaining of a mind in the moment presence, and their engagement in self-evaluation: the athlete as a *performer*.

When considering this definition of the positive mental health of an athlete, it becomes apparent that the mental and emotional development of the athlete—that is, a bedrock of mental health—can be seen at three separate yet interrelated levels:

1. *Individual level*: At this level, the focus for fostering positive athlete mental health centers on assessing their mental health needs as a person, particularly in terms of how they cope with risk, how they relate to others, and how they make sense of their performance.
2. *Team level*: At this level, the focus of mental health is on creating a team environment that is supportive of the mental health needs of all team members, including not only the needs of athletes but also those of coaches and staff.
3. *Organizational level*: At this level, the focus of mental health is on leadership and communication regarding policies, programs, and best practices that support positive mental health for all athletes, coaches, and staff.

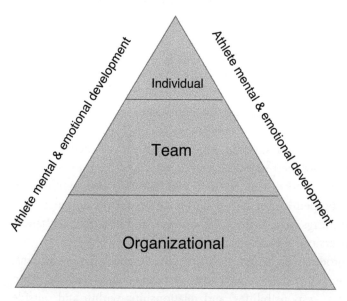

Figure 1.1 Levels of Athlete Mental and Emotional Development

When working with athletes, coaches, and staff to support their mental health, a systems approach considers all these stakeholders as important and necessary. This kind of approach provides us, as practitioners, with flexibility and a broad-based perspective that encompasses many relevant factors we need to consider as part of our work with athletes, coaches, and staff.

RISK AND PROTECTIVE FACTORS IN SPORT ORGANIZATIONS

When we consider mental health in sport organizations at individual, team, and organizational levels, we can identify a range of human and systemic factors that influence how the athlete uses their thoughts, emotions, and actions. Consequently, this systems approach realization provides guidance concerning how coaches, staff, and others can be actively involved in identifying both risk and factors that mitigate risks. That is, we can identify risk factors that place the athlete, team, and organization at risk for mental health problems and concerns. In addition, protective factors that are protective or supportive of mental health at these levels also can become apparent (Arnold & Fletcher, 2012).

Risk factors are people, places, things, and circumstances that, if left unchecked, can increase the probability of the occurrence of mental health problems in athletes, coaches, and staff (Gouttebarge et al., 2019). In contrast, protective factors are conditions that support the mental and emotional development of the athlete, thereby mitigating risk related to anything that can spur mental health problems (Keyes, 2007). For the most part, protective factors are similar in nature and scope to indicators that serve to promote positive athlete mental health, such as being able to effectively balance sport with the rest of their life, having self-confidence and composure, being a good teammate, and possessing high self-esteem.

By taking a systems approach concerning what factors either inhibit or facilitate positive mental health in sport organizations, we can identify risk and protective factors, respectively, at individual, team, and organizational levels. In this sense, it is important for us as practitioners to come to know what these factors may be in the sport settings in which we work.

There are a range of factors that can place an athlete, coach, or staff member in a sport organization at risk for mental health problems. These risk factors include but are not limited to the following:

- Academic problems and failures that keep an athlete out of competition.
- Difficulties paying attention to the requirements of school and other tasks, perhaps related to attention deficit disorder and/or hyperactivity.
- Improper use of substances, including banned substances.
- Discouragement over being demoted to a lower team.
- Orthopedic injuries and other medical illnesses, particularly those involving long-term physical rehabilitation.
- Poor work habits before and following performances.
- Stressful life experiences.
- Poor athletic performance.
- Anger and other forms of emotional deregulation.

In contrast, other factors are protective and supportive in nature and scope and can contribute to the positive mental health of the athlete. These protective factors include but are not limited to the following:

- Possession of a clear sense of values and purpose.
- Awareness of their strong points and developmental needs as an athlete.
- Self-motivation to be the best version of themselves possible.
- Belief in their capacity to compete and execute during competition.
- Capacity to make healthy life choices and decisions.
- Social and emotional support from family and other relevant stakeholders.
- Good physical strength and condition.
- Ability to interact productively and appropriately with others.

Risk and Protective Factors at the *Team Level*

At the team level, there are risk and protective factors also relevant for athletes, the team, and its environment. Team-level risk factors likely related to mental health include the following:

Charting the Parameters of Mental Health in Sport Organizations

- Lack of clarity and awareness of team purpose and goals.
- Poor team cohesion and team relationships.
- Ready access to drugs, performance-enhancing substances, and/or alcohol, as well as encouragement to use them.
- Stress and demands concerning practices and workout load.
- Limited communication with coaches and others.
- Discrimination, both racial and otherwise.
- Dismissal of attempts for the team to discuss mental health.
- Lack of mental health literacy.

In contrast, other factors at the team level are likely to support the maintenance of positive mental health. These are *protective factors* and may include the following:

- Clarity and buy-in regarding team purpose and goals.
- Productive and appropriate interaction between and among teammates.
- Sense of trust with coaches and support staff members.
- Respect for one's culture, ethnicity, and linguistic development.
- Willingness to talk about mental health.
- Access to mental health (referrals and services).
- Clarity concerning issues of confidentiality.
- Assistance for dealing with drug and substance abuse issues.

Risk and Protective Factors at the *Organizational Level*

When a sport organization embraces a systems approach toward mental health, it becomes readily apparent that there are risk and protective factors also operating at that level. Here are important organizational-level *risk factors* to recognize:

- Department directors and other leaders do not discuss or even consider mental health in relation to athletes.
- There is evident resistance to fund and support mental health initiatives.
- Organizational leaders, coaches, and support staff are illiterate about the nature and scope of athlete mental health.
- No written policies or plans pertinent to mental health have been formulated.
- Athletes and staff have limited access to mental health services.

In contrast, there are several organizational-level *protective factors*. These include:

- Leadership considers the fostering of the mental health of athletes, coaches, and others as an important, strategic priority.
- Resources are readily available to support mental health education and intervention services for athletes and others.
- Policies, plans, and procedures are documented and discussed with coaches and athletes.
- Qualified mental health providers are in place to provide needed services.

If we are going to contribute to fostering positive mental health of athletes, coaches, and staff in sport organizations, our recognition of risk and protective factors can benefit us in several ways. Our recognition can lead to awareness of specific things that can influence the mental health of athletes and others. In addition, we can uncover opportunities to communicate with coaches and administrators about the foundations of a mentally healthy sport organization, and we can use information about risk and protective factors as a basis for the development of mental health programs.

SOME IMPORTANT TERMS AND THEIR RELATIONSHIPS TO ONE ANOTHER

Throughout the chapters of this book, there will be discussion about and reference to "mental skills," "life skills," and "mental health" in sport organizations. There also will be discussion about the "mental and emotional development" of the athlete. At this point, it is useful to define and distinguish these terms since our understanding of the terms influences how we proceed to support the mental health of the athlete.

Mental and emotional development has to do with how the athlete learns to use their thoughts, emotions, and actions so that they can be the best version possible of themselves as a person, coper, teammate, and performer (Maher, 2011, 2021a). I effectively have explained this to athletes and others by using the acronym TEA: thoughts, emotions, and actions. Their TEAs are their personal assets or their liabilities, depending on how they proceed to use them both within and outside competitive venues. Positive mental and emotional development signifies the athlete is learning to maximize their TEAs as an asset.

Mental skills reflect thoughts, emotions, and actions that can assist athletes in maintaining and enhancing their performance. From my experiences, important mental skills that athletes have found to be helpful include goal setting, visualization (imagery), self-talk, energy activation, focus and attention control, deep breathing, and progressive relaxation. Mental skills coaches and sport psychologists provide mental skills programs and services that deal with competitive matters, typically related to the court or field.

Life skills reflect thoughts, emotions, and actions that assist athletes in making effective choices and healthy decisions pertaining to their lives outside competitive venues. Life skills may include mindfulness, sound nutritional habits, making informed decisions about the use of substances, proper hydration, routines for meaningful sleep and recovery, and financial literacy and management. Life skills are best taught to athletes by professionals who are qualified in the respective areas of living.

Mental health, as discussed in a prior section of this chapter, involves the psychological, emotional, and social well-being of athletes. An athlete's mental health relates to their understanding of themselves as a person, as an individual who can cope effectively with risk, as a teammate, and as a performer. Toward those ends, athletes will call on a range of mental skills, life skills, and other skills, all of which can contribute to positive mental health. (As they do so, they demonstrate positive mental and emotional development.)

The notion of *mental and emotional outcomes* also is important to note here, since these outcomes are indicators of positive mental health in athletes, coaches, and others (Maher, 2021b). The mental and emotional outcomes I have found to be useful in monitoring athletes (and coaches and staff) and their development, both within and outside competitive venues, consist of the following:

- *Perspective:* balancing sport with life.
- *Personal awareness:* knowing one's strong points and needs for development.
- *Self-motivation:* enthusiastic pursuit of important, meaningful goals.
- *Mental discipline:* following through on plans and commitments.

Table 1.1 Mental and Emotional Outcomes

	Strong	Weak	Other Comments
Perspective			
Personal awareness			
Self-motivation			
Mental discipline			
Self-confidence			
Emotional intensity			
Focus			
Composure			
Teamwork			
Self-esteem			
Performance accountability			
Continuous improvement			

- *Self-confidence:* believing in the capacity to compete and execute.
- *Emotional intensity:* engaging in sport with effective energy and effort.
- *Focus:* paying attention to what matters at the moment.
- *Composure:* remaining calm during challenging circumstances.
- *Teamwork:* interacting productively with others.
- *Self-esteem:* valuing oneself as a person over and above performance.
- *Performance accountability:* being responsible for what one can control.
- *Continuous improvement:* seeking to get better, one step at a time.

NATURE, SCOPE, AND INDICATORS OF A MENTALLY HEALTHY SPORT ORGANIZATION

I have used the term "mentally healthy sport organization" as part of the subtitle of the book, and I will be using this term throughout the book. Therefore, it is incumbent on me to discuss the meaning of this term and how I have come to define and use it.

There is no definition of what constitutes a mentally healthy sport organization, nor is there research about and discussion of that notion in professional psychology literature, as far as I am aware. Yet, based on my 33 years of professional practice in sport, performance, and organizational psychology, I know it is very helpful to me—and meaningful to many organizational stakeholders—to use the term mentally healthy sport organization. Over the years, I have had the privilege of working with many outstanding human beings (athletes, coaches, staff, and administrators) in a range of sport organizations. In working with them to support mental health in their organizational settings, many of them, in one way or another, have asked me how to develop their organization so that mental health is built into it as an integral aspect of organizational culture and routine. Some of these stakeholders have had prior negative experiences with mental health initiatives and regretted that mental health of athletes had become a marginalized aspect of their organization.

In responding to these kinds of requests, I have come to understand, recognize, and appreciate that there are a range of indicators that allow us to consider a sport organization a mentally healthy one. Relatedly, and most important, I am convinced that unless a sport organization is structured (organized) in a purposeful and strategic manner to foster mental health for all its stakeholders, it will fail to recognize and thus lose opportunities to provide mental health programs, services, and other related initiatives. Missed opportunities to foster mental health in a sport organization are indeed unfortunate; had they been aware of the possibilities for an organization to foster mental health, practitioners and others could have taken advantage of these opportunities.

So, what is a practical and meaningful way to proceed to develop a mentally healthy sport organization? To start, consideration must be given to what constitutes a "sport organization." I define a sport organization as a structured, purposeful entity in which athletes are engaged in skillful mental and physical effort as individuals and teammates, according to performance standards, rules, and procedures, being guided by coaches, staff, and administrators. Based on this definition, many types of sport organizations can be identified. These include professional sport franchises, college and university divisions of athletics, secondary school athletic departments, and sport academies.

As I have worked in various sport organizations to foster mental health, I have formulated a set of quality indicators that seem to be associated with sport organizations that have valuable mental health programs, services, plans, and procedures. These quality indicators mark a sport organization as mentally healthy. In providing these indicators, I fully recognize that a sport organization will not be able to meet all these indicators at any one point in time. However, a mentally healthy organization can be developed using these indicators as a guide (and with the use of a systems approach that will be described in the next chapter).

If you are working with the intent to develop a mentally healthy sport organization—one where athletes, coaches, and staff are provided valuable mental health programs and services—consider these 15 indicators (which also will be covered in subsequent chapters of the book):

1. Leadership considers the mental health of athletes, coaches, and staff to be an integral part of the sport organization.
2. Adequate funding is available to support mental health initiatives within the context of the sport organization.
3. Qualified, licensed mental health professionals, along with other contributors, have been hired or contracted to provide mental health programs and services.
4. The qualified, licensed mental health professionals and other contributors intend to consider athletes, coaches, and staff as performers and people regarding their mental and emotional development.
5. A clear and compelling vision has been communicated to all relevant stakeholders about the mental health of athletes and others in relation to individual, team, and organizational levels.
6. Fostering mental health is seen as being a multidisciplinary, proactive endeavor, rather than a reactive and narrow search for psychopathology.
7. Key leaders and other contributors are actively involved in overseeing the mental health area so that best practices are utilized.
8. There is an ongoing process for the assessment of the mental health needs of athletes, coaches, and staff; this assessment information serves as a basis for the design and implementation of programs and services that are valuable and have merit.
9. Mental health programs and services are designed and implemented based on needs assessment results.
10. Coaches, staff, and administrators are educated and trained about mental health so that they can be aware of the subject and act in support of athletes and their needs and circumstances.

Table 1.2 Indicators for Developing a Mentally Healthy Sport Organization

	Present	Absent	Needs Improvement/Comments
Leadership support			
Adequate funding			
Mental health professionals			
Athletes, etc., as performers and people			
Clearly communicated vision			
Multidisciplinary, proactive endeavor			
Key leaders and best practices			
Ongoing assessment process			
Programs and services based on needs			
Leaders educated and trained			
Conducive team environment			
Policies, plans, and procedures support mental health			
Mental health, mental skills, and life skills coordinated			
Evaluation process established			
Program evaluation information communicated and utilized			

11. A team environment conducive to mental health is established.
12. Policies, plans, and procedures are formulated and enacted to support mental health, including response to mental health crises and emergencies.

13. Mental health is coordinated in an effective manner with the mental skills and life skills domains.
14. There is a process for evaluating how mental health programs and services have benefited athletes, coaches, and staff in terms of their mental and emotional development and well-being.
15. Program evaluation information about mental health is both communicated to relevant parties and used as a basis for continuous program improvement.

Practitioner Exercises

1. What have been your philosophy and beliefs about the mental health of athletes? Consider how consistent you have been in communicating these philosophies and beliefs to yourself and others. Pinpoint where and how you might gain further clarity about the topic of athlete mental health.
2. How active have you been in the support of the mental health of coaches, support staff, and administrators? Think about how you can look at these individuals and groups as part of your client base. Then, if appropriate, formulate a plan of action for adding them to your practice.
3. Evaluate yourself regarding your current practice, and reflect on how you can contribute to mental health in sport organizations. What do you need to get better at or learn more about? How might you fill those gaps, or what resources do you need to improve and learn more?

Two

This chapter provides an overview of a systems approach practitioners can use to deal productively with the task of fostering the mental health of athletes and others in sport organizations. First, it offers a rationale for how a systems approach can be a valuable investment of practitioner time, thought, and action when addressing the mental health needs of athletes, coaches, and staff through mental health programs and services. Second, the chapter discusses the nature and scope of the systems approach and its helpfulness in developing a mentally healthy sport organization. Third, it delineates the framework and constituent dimensions of the systems approach. Fourth, it sets forth the steps that comprise the systems approach. The chapter concludes with practitioner exercises.

RATIONALE FOR A SYSTEMS APPROACH TO MENTAL HEALTH IN SPORT ORGANIZATIONS

Sport organizations exist in many sizes, structures, and locations in the United States and worldwide (Arnold & Fletcher, 2012). This is the case at professional, collegiate, and secondary school levels. However, no matter the size, structure, and location of a sport organization, it likely considers mental health an important aspect of its organization, now more than ever (Fletcher et al., 2003). Moreover, within a sport organizational context, mental health is important not only for athletes, but also for coaches, staff, and administrators (Maher, 2021b).

An increase in the recognition of the importance of mental health is indeed encouraging. Despite this trend, though, the task of fostering mental health in a sport organization typically has focused on the assessment and treatment of the mental health problems of an individual athlete—which, of course, is an important focus. However, the matter of mental health in a sport organization also involves other organizational stakeholders besides athletes, particularly coaches, athletic trainers, strength and conditioning staff, sport administrators, and teams.

DOI: 10.4324/9781003159018-2

I have been practicing sport and performance psychology in a range of sport organizations, large and small in nature and scope, for 33 years. I have come to realize more and more that mental health initiatives in sport organizations require multidisciplinary teamwork and attention to a range of human and systemic factors. This is because mental health initiatives occur at many levels, affect many people, and cut across a range of units of a sport organization. Thus, it is not surprising that practitioners of sport psychology will find it necessary to take a systems view when they are seeking to design and implement mental health programs and services for a range of target populations (athletes, coaches, staff). Without multidisciplinary teamwork and a broad-based view of the sport organization, the mental health programs and services the practitioner provides may well be limited in nature, scope, and relevance. If thus limited, athletes and other stakeholders will be shortchanged (Dominici, 2012).

Accordingly, if it considers athletes as well as other stakeholders, a mentally healthy sport organization can be a worthwhile entity for all concerned. As discussed in more detail in Chapter 1, a mentally healthy sport organization can be configured across various areas of mental health (prevention, education, treatment) and at different levels (individual, team, organizational). Indeed, mental health in a sport organization impacts athletes, coaches, and staff as individuals, as teams, and within larger contexts.

A systems approach targeted to developing a mentally healthy sport organization will benefit all concerned. A systems approach enables the practitioner to view interrelationships at individual, team, and organizational levels and with respect to a range of target populations (athletes, coaches, staff). A systems vantage point creates opportunity to consider—and act on—a range of factors that affect mental health needs and mental health services delivery. (These factors include relevant social, political, cultural, ethnic, and organizational factors.) In addition, a systems approach stands in contrast to approaches that focus solely on the individual athlete, since the latter often does not consider other levels, factors, and contexts important to the individual's mental health in the sport organization.

NATURE AND SCOPE OF A SYSTEMS APPROACH

A systems approach is a way of viewing an organization with the intent of better understanding it and developing it (Maher, 2012). In management, education, and other human service domains, the notion of a systems approach burgeoned during the 1960s. Ludwig von Bertalanffy and George Miller served as major contributors to its conceptualization and use (Meadows, 2008).

A systems approach reflects the way a practitioner proceeds in considering an organization as a system, that is, as a set of parts (subsystems) that interact with and are interdependent on one another (Arnold & Wade, 2015). Relatedly, and most important, a systems approach helps broaden a focus on developing and maintaining a mentally healthy organization (Maher, 2021a).

I have found the use of a systems approach to be a valuable aspect of my professional practice within the contexts of sport organizations at professional and collegiate levels. For me and for other practitioners of sport psychology who work in sport organizations in areas of mental health and mental performance, the systems approach has the following benefits:

- The sport organization is viewed as a set of interacting units, all of which have relevance to the mental health and mental performance of athletes, coaches, and staff. These organizational units may include the strength and conditioning area, the sports medicine department, sport psychology services, player technical skills sections, and staff development domains.
- People recognize that the sport organization encompasses a hierarchical structure, particularly at individual, team, and organizational levels of operation.

When the task is to foster the mental health of athletes, coaches, and staff in a sport organization, a systems approach provides these guidelines for practitioners of sport psychology:

- Mental health programs and services are viewed as a service delivery system, highlighting the importance of coordination across programs and services.

- A mental health service delivery system, comprising programs and services, has separate yet interrelated levels: individual, team, and organizational.
- The programs and services that make up a mental health service delivery system have a common purpose: enhancing the mental and emotional development of those who are part of the system—athletes, coaches, staff—not only as performers but also as people.

A systems approach places a premium on fostering mental health in a sport organization in a step-by-step manner. The use of a systems approach allows practitioners to address the mental health needs of athletes and others in relation to individual, team, and organizational levels. In this book, I characterize a systems approach for developing a mentally healthy sport organization by the following qualities:

- The task of fostering the mental health of athletes, coaches, and staff in a sport organization is a multidisciplinary one; it occurs across various people and levels.
- The systems approach is organized by a set of sequential, interrelated steps that address important factors, thus enabling practitioners to design and implement mental health programs and services based on needs of athletes, coaches, and staff.
- A systems approach draws focus to distinct levels of intervention, particularly individual, team, and organizational levels.
- Within a systems perspective, practitioners rely on evaluation information to make decisions about mental health in the organization and the direction of its programs, services, and related initiatives.

FRAMEWORK OF THE SYSTEMS APPROACH

The systems approach, which is the framework for this book, intends to contribute to three tasks:

- Developing a mentally healthy sport organization.
- Fostering the mental health of athletes, coaches, and others by making sure programs and services address priority mental health needs of athletes and others.

- Seeking to assure that mental health programs and services are provided at individual, team, and organizational levels, based on needs assessment information.

The systems approach for developing a mentally healthy sport organization consists of three separate yet interrelated dimensions. These dimensions are seen visually as a matrix in Table 2.1. These dimensions are:

1. *Levels of intervention*: the vertical dimension of the matrix.
2. *Process of practice*: the horizontal dimension of the matrix.
3. *Programs and services*: the cells of the matrix.

Levels of Intervention (Vertical Dimension of the Matrix)

This dimension of the systems approach refers to the levels at which mental health programs and services can be provided to athletes, coaches, and others. It is the vertical dimension of the matrix seen in Table 2.1. We can call these programs and services mental health interventions. The value of the systems approach in fostering mental health in the sport organization is that it considers the various levels of intervention for programs and services. These levels are:

- *Individual level*: At this level, the interventions not only address the mental health needs of the individual athlete through an individualized program, but they also consider the mental health needs of other possible stakeholders, including coaches and team managers, athletic trainers, strength and conditioning coaches, physical therapists, department heads, and athletic administrators.
- *Team level*: At this level, the focus is on the creation of a team environment so that athletes, coaches, and staff—all those for whom

Table 2.1 Three Dimensions of the Systems Approach

	Clarification	Design	Implementation	Evaluation
Individual level				
Team level				
Organizational level				

mental health programs and services are available—find it safe to discuss mental health.

- *Organizational level:* This level includes the development, coordination, and enactment of organization-wide policies, plans, and procedures that support mental health at the individual and team levels.

Process of Practice (Horizontal Dimension of the Matrix)

This dimension of the systems approach highlights the importance of providing mental health programs and services in a step-by-step manner. This process of practice is the horizontal dimension of the matrix in Table 2.1. In short, this process of practice is the way the practitioner (such as you or I) works regarding mental health when we use the systems approach. This dimension includes the following phases:

- *Clarification:* This phase involves gathering information and making judgments about the mental health needs of athletes and others at the individual, team, and organizational levels. It also includes obtaining organizational readiness information about the relevant context in which those needs are embedded.
- *Design:* This phase involves designing mental health programs and services based on needs of athletes and others and making sure that each program has purpose, goals, and activities that can be implemented and evaluated.
- *Implementation:* This level reflects the monitoring of the program or service to determine if it is being implemented as designed.
- *Evaluation:* This level has to do with undertaking program evaluation activities and making judgments about the implementation and value of mental health programs and services, including when and how to adjust them.

Programs and Services (the Cells of the Matrix)

This dimension of the systems approach signifies the methods and procedures that are used across each phase of the process and at each level. (See the cells of the matrix in Table 2.1.) This dimension of the systems approach allows the practitioner to be both proactive and active in linking assessment information to programs and services.

This dimension also allows the practitioner to proceed in a step-by-step manner. Based on the use of the matrix in Table 2.1, I have identified 12 steps the practitioner can take to foster mental health in a sport organization as they pursue developing a mentally healthy organizational entity. While this chapter presents an overview of the steps, remaining chapters of the book will flesh them out in more detail.

TWELVE STEPS TO CONSIDER FOR THE PRACTITIONER FROM A SYSTEMS PERSPECTIVE

I have found it important to take the following steps to foster mental health and develop a mentally healthy sport organization. My colleagues and I have successfully engaged these steps in a range of professional and collegiate sport organizations. These steps were derived from the systems approach matrix discussed above.

The 12 steps are as follows:

1. Create a compelling vision for developing a mentally healthy sport organization.
2. Understand the readiness of the sport organization for taking on mental health initiatives.
3. Identify and hire qualified, licensed mental health professionals.
4. Describe the target populations who will receive the mental health programs and services.
5. Assess the mental health needs of athletes, coaches, and staff, preparing to use the needs as a basis for program design and implementation.
6. Design and implement mental health programs and services, based on needs assessment results.
7. Educate and train coaches, staff, and administrators about mental health.
8. Establish a team environment in support of mental health.
9. Formulate and enact organizational policies, plans, and procedures.
10. Coordinate mental skills, life skills, and mental health programs.
11. Evaluate mental health programs and services.
12. Communicate information about the value of mental health to relevant stakeholders.

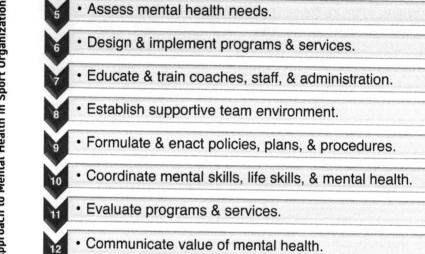

1. • Create vision.

2. • Understand readiness.

3. • Identify & hire mental health professionals.

4. • Describe target populations.

5. • Assess mental health needs.

6. • Design & implement programs & services.

7. • Educate & train coaches, staff, & administration.

8. • Establish supportive team environment.

9. • Formulate & enact policies, plans, & procedures.

10. • Coordinate mental skills, life skills, & mental health.

11. • Evaluate programs & services.

12. • Communicate value of mental health.

Figure 2.1 Steps Derived from a Systems Perspective

Practitioner Exercises

1. Recall your experiences in working as a practitioner in a sport organization. What are the predominant ways athletes, coaches, and staff have perceived the mental health domain? Have their perceptions focused on the individual level only or included other levels? To what extent have you been involved in fostering the mental health of athletes and others in sport organizations? What have you learned from these experiences?

2. As you seek to use a systems approach in your sport psychology practice in sport organizations, what are likely factors

that could inhibit your use of this kind of approach? What can you do to minimize these factors?

3. How can the systems approach described in this chapter allow you to enhance your work in the mental health domain in sport organizations? How can you leverage such possibilities?

4. For what reasons might a sport organization have marginalized mental health? To what extent have you experienced this kind of phenomenon? To what extent have you been pleased or dissatisfied with these experiences?

5. Consider the current organization in which you work as a sport psychology practitioner. Decide how you would proceed to communicate the value of a systems approach as a basis for fostering the mental health of athletes, coaches, and staff. To whom would you communicate this information?

6. Of the 12 steps described in this chapter, which ones are you most likely to be able to take and complete successfully? Why? Which steps would present a challenge? Why?

Three

This chapter provides information about how to develop, document, and articulate a clear vision about mental health for a sport organization. Such a vision statement can serve as direction for developing positive mental health programs and services within a sport organizational context. A vision statement also can be a springboard for clarifying directions for practitioners about how to proceed in realizing the vision at individual, team, and organizational levels. First, the chapter offers a rationale explaining what a vision statement signifies for athletes, coaches, and staff. Second, it discusses the benefits of a vision statement. Third, it considers how to create and solidify a vision statement for a sport organization, with an emphasis on the use of a multidisciplinary committee. Fourth, the chapter shares guidelines concerning how and with whom a vision statement can be shared. The guidelines also will suggest how to leverage the statement for moving ahead with the task of fostering mental health in the sport organization. Finally, the end of the chapter includes practitioner exercises.

RATIONALE FOR A VISION ABOUT MENTAL HEALTH

It is not that easy a task to initiate a focus on, and a direction for, mental health in a sport organization. Although many factors can limit such an attempt, one area that requires clarification is the definition of "mental health" (Vella et al., 2021). Clarifying the nature and scope of mental health is important, particularly in a sport organization. Unless it is clear what you mean by mental health, the term can be confusing or misleading to athletes, coaches, staff, and others.

When I have asked athletes and coaches at professional and collegiate levels what mental health means to them, I have received a wide range of responses. These responses have included comments about mental health such as: mental health occurs when the athlete is not ill

DOI: 10.4324/9781003159018-3

or unstable; the athlete who has mental health is not depressed or anxious; the athlete with good mental health is mentally tough; and the mentally healthy athlete is able to balance their sport with their life.

Once clarity exists about the nature and scope of mental health, however, the psychological conditions are set so that everyone will be on the same wavelength about what is meant by the term (Cruickshank & Collins, 2012). Without this shared definition, any attempts at moving ahead with mental health initiatives and developing a mentally healthy sport organization may very well be limited in actions, in collaboration, and in what can be accomplished in terms of mental and emotional development. The task of clearly defining mental health, therefore, demands thought and attention as well as clear and thoughtful written information (Henriksen et al., 2020).

If a practitioner (like you) intends to develop a range of mental health initiatives that can become an integral part of a sport organization, then establishing a vision about mental health is a good start. In this regard, the notion of mental health is the vision—the why and what—while mental health initiatives—the how and when—follow from the vision. A useful definition for a "mental health initiative" is a program, service, activity, or event that seeks to foster the mental health of athletes or other relevant stakeholders such as coaches, staff, and athletic administrators. We will be discussing a range of mental health initiatives, particularly programs and services, in subsequent chapters of the book.

BENEFITS OF A VISION ABOUT MENTAL HEALTH

A clear, thoughtfully crafted vision about mental health, presented as a written vision statement, functions as a basic starting point for promoting positive mental health in a sport organization. A vision statement has the following benefits:

- Signifies to athletes, coaches, and staff that the sport organization considers their mental health important not only to them as performers but also as people, over and above sport—that is, the total individual as both performer and person.
- Emphasizes that the sport organization intends to develop programs and services that will foster positive mental health.

- Explicates the meaning of mental health for athletes as well as for other relevant stakeholders.
- Sets the conditions so that athletes, coaches, and staff communicate with one another about mental health at individual, team, and organizational levels.
- Offers a perspective that mental health is an important state to seek and is not simply an absence of mental illness.
- Mentions explicitly that a range of stakeholders desire to develop a mentally healthy sport organization.

NATURE AND SCOPE OF A MENTAL HEALTH VISION STATEMENT

It is useful to present a vision about mental health within the context of a sport organization in written form. You can refer to this document as a vision statement. It can include, but not be limited to, the following elements:

- Acknowledgment of the need for attention to mental health in sports.
- Reasons why the present time is an important time to address mental health in the sport organization.
- Recognition of the range of stakeholders for whom mental health programs and services can be of value.
- Clarification of what mental health is and is not.
- Description of procedures for communication and collaboration regarding athlete mental health.
- Specific instructions regarding how to proceed with fostering mental health in the organization.

Drafting a Mental Health Vision Statement

You can produce a draft of a mental health vision statement if you are serving as a program or mental health consultant to a sport organization. Alternatively, a multidisciplinary mental health committee—on which you may serve as chair or facilitator—may develop a vision statement. (The use of such a committee will be described below.)

You can follow a set of steps as you draft a mental health vision statement. I have found the following steps useful when collaborating with coaches and administrators seeking to promote positive mental health in their respective sport organization:

1. Provide an overview or definition of the meaning of mental health.
2. Emphasize the importance of mental health for the sport organization and its stakeholders (athletes, coaches, staff).
3. State the intentions of the sport organization regarding mental health.
4. Identify the professionals who will be involved in fostering positive mental health in the sport organization.
5. Mention how, where, and when mental health programs and services may occur.
6. Inform any recipients of the draft statement how they can offer comments and feedback about the mental health vision statement.

Here is an example of a mental health vision statement developed in a collegiate athletic department using the above steps:

> Mental health of our student-athletes is a priority area for their overall well-being and for the continued development of the department. Relatedly, the mental health of our coaches and staff also is an important matter and departmental responsibility. When seen in a positive perspective, mental health is considered as reflecting

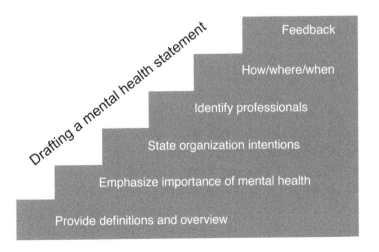

Figure 3.1 Steps in Drafting a Mental Health Statement

the psychological, emotional, and social well-being of our student-athletes, coaches, and staff. The task of fostering their mental health is the responsibility of all of us who work at individual, team, and organizational levels. During the forthcoming months, our intention is to develop programs and services that will contribute to making our athletic department united about mental health and lead to a mentally healthy sport organization.

Similarly, here is an example of a mental health vision statement for a professional basketball franchise. In this situation, I took the lead in formulating the statement with the help of a mental health task force:

Our players constitute our most important resource; they are valuable human beings to us and their families. We want to make sure each player develops to be the best version of their being, as a performer and person. One priority area for player development is that of mental health. Mental health means our players are growing and developing, mentally and emotionally, on and off the court, and that they are effective in coping with the demands they encounter. As a professional basketball organization, it is our intention to support the mental health not only of our players but also that of our staff. We intend to do this by educating players, coaches, and staff about mental health and by providing them with qualified resources they can access to address mental health needs.

Utilization of a Mental Health Committee

When creating a mental health vision statement as a basis for providing direction for promoting positive mental health in a sport organization, I have found it very helpful to form and utilize a mental health committee or task force. (The exact term to call this group will depend on the preferences of the sport organization.) The purpose of a mental health committee is to provide a vision and direction for the task of fostering positive mental health in the sport organization. Besides being involved in the creation of a mental health vision statement, the committee also can be involved with many other steps and activities (covered in subsequent chapters of the book).

The committee can include representatives from various areas of the sport organization. Given its purpose, the committee likely will function effectively with 8–11 members. These members could include:

- Athletic trainer.
- Mental skills coach.
- Strength and conditioning staff member.
- Three athletic coaches.
- Sport administrator.
- One or two athletes.
- One or two licensed mental health providers (perhaps you), with one of them serving as chair.

The responsibilities of the committee include:

- Create a vision statement about mental health that will be meaningful to athletes, coaches, and staff of the organization.
- Communicate a vision about mental health that is compelling and meaningful to all relevant organizational stakeholders.
- Provide suggestions for the identification and development of mental health programs and services in the organization that can be implemented over the course of time.
- Review the mental health programs and services in the process of being developed as well as those that have been implemented.
- Fulfill any other committee responsibilities.

COMMUNICATION OF A VISION FOR MENTAL HEALTH

Once you or a committee have formulated a vision statement, you or the mental health committee can communicate the statement to relevant stakeholders of the sport organization. Communication of the vision statement to relevant stakeholders is intended to make clear the following:

- Mental health is a priority in the sport organization.
- The sport organization intends to provide resources to foster the mental health of athletes and others.
- The direction the organization will take in promoting positive mental health begins with determining the kinds of programs and

services that will enable the development and maintenance of a mentally healthy sport organization.

You can communicate your vision by sending the vision statement to the stakeholders. Follow that communication with an opportunity for stakeholders to engage in a real-time discussion about the vision statement and directions for mental health in the organization. Such discussion should result in the stakeholders acquiring specific understanding about the notion of mental health and the direction for mental health programs and services in the organization.

Practitioner Exercises

1. Ask athletes and coaches with whom you work about the nature and scope of mental health. (This type of interaction can occur either individually or in a group format.) In particular, try to find out what the term "mental health" means to them. Relatedly, discuss with them what they think a mental health program geared toward their needs and those of others should include. Use this kind of feedback to inform yourself and others about how athletes and coaches think about mental health.

2. Take time to examine your own beliefs and opinions about the area of mental health in relation to athletes and sport organizations. In so doing, identify areas or issues about which you are unsure or need to learn more. Use this examination to decide how you can continue your education about the mental health domain.

3. Discuss the area of mental health and sport with a practitioner experienced in this area. Let them talk about their experiences, both the good experiences and those that are not so good. Ask them what they have learned from these experiences.

4. Recall your own experiences with seeking to promote mental health in sport organizations. What do you think went well with your efforts, and why? What did not happen as you expected? What have you or what can you now learn from those experiences?

Four

This chapter reviews the assessment of the readiness of a sport organization for mental health initiatives; it also provides guidelines for practitioners to conduct such an organizational readiness assessment. First, the chapter gives a definition of a mental health initiative and of a sport organization so that it will be clear to all concerned what needs to be considered when assessing sport organizational readiness for mental health initiatives. Second, it presents the notion of organizational readiness, including how this form of assessment applies to a sport organization. Third, it identifies specific factors associated with the readiness of a sport organization for mental health initiatives. Fourth, the chapter discusses methods to assess the readiness factors and gathers assessment information. Fifth, it sets forth guidelines that will provide practitioners with methods to make judgments about organizational readiness for mental health programs, services, and related activities. Practitioner exercises conclude the chapter.

DEFINITION OF A MENTAL HEALTH INITIATIVE

The task of fostering mental health in a sport organization is an important one for the practitioner and all other relevant stakeholders. However, in order to be a worthwhile investment of time and effort, this task requires thought, clarity, and definition at individual, team, and organizational levels (Damschroder et al., 2009). Without such clarity and perspective, it will be very difficult, if not impossible, to get started with fostering the mental health of athletes, coaches, and others. Furthermore, the challenge to sustain any efforts will be limited, over the short-term and longer haul, regarding mental health in a sport organization (Maher, 2021a).

In the last chapter, we discussed creating a vision statement about mental health. The vision statement serves as a basis for thinking about

DOI: 10.4324/9781003159018-4

and deciding directions for mental health initiatives. In this chapter, we are going to discuss how to assess the readiness of a sport organization for mental health initiatives. Before doing so, however, it is necessary that we define this notion—mental health initiative—clearly.

There is no uniform definition of a "mental health initiative," although the term initiative has been used in various ways in a range of settings and circumstances. Based on my professional practice and work in fostering mental health in sport organizations, I have created and used this definition of a mental health initiative in a range of sport organizations at professional and collegiate levels:

- A *mental health initiative* is a program, service, event, or activity that relates to mental health in a sport organization. A mental health initiative is intended to enhance the mental health and well-being of athletes, coaches, and staff, thereby contributing to their development as performers and people. A mental health initiative occurs within the context of the sport organization, and it is supportive of the organization's overall mission for athletics.

When unpacking this definition of a mental health initiative, many specific points become apparent:

- The definition allows for a wide range of activities to fall under the scope of mental health initiatives. These possibilities could include, for instance: (a) mental health programs that are educational, preventative, or skill-building in nature and scope; (b) mental health services intended to help athletes and others who manifest mental health concerns and problems; (c) mental performance programs; (d) events such as a mental health awareness day; (e) planned activities, such as mental health literacy training; and (f) mental health fundraising ventures.
- Mental health initiatives each have distinct purposes and goals; at least, they should have them. Mental health initiatives are intended to initiate and foster mental health, and they are conducted within a sport organizational context.
- Mental health initiatives are linked to the overall mission of the sport organization. These programs, services, events, and activities

should be an integral part of the sport organization. Thus, the organization provides them not only for athletes but also for other target populations such as coaches, staff, and athletic administrators.

DEFINITION OF A SPORT ORGANIZATION

Just as the term mental health initiative requires definition, so too does the term "sport organization." In other words, to assess the readiness of a sport organization regarding mental health initiatives, it is essential to be clear about the nature and scope of a sport organization (Wagstaff, 2017). I define a sport organization as an entity that meets the following criteria:

- It delineates a mission and set of goals that guide organizational efforts and that focus on the development of its athletes—physically, mentally, emotionally, and technically.
- The organization includes one or more sports as part of the organization.
- The well-being and performance of athletes are central to the organization.
- The sport organization employs or contracts with coaches and support staff, such as athletic trainers and sport psychologists.
- The organization provides coaches and staff with information, equipment, and facilities so they can engage in their roles effectively.
- The organization formulates and enacts policies and procedures to administer and supervise the activities of the athletes, coaches, and others.

Based on that understanding of the nature and scope, there are various kinds of "sport organizations." These include, but are not limited to, the following examples:

- Professional sport franchise.
- Division of intercollegiate athletics.
- Department of sports medicine.
- Sport academy for elite athletes.
- High school athletic department.

ORGANIZATIONAL READINESS

In order to assess the readiness of a sport organization for mental health initiatives, we must understand what is meant by organizational "readiness." Otherwise, what is going to be assessed will not be clear. This lack of clarity may very well serve to limit support for mental health in the sport organization and to undermine the larger task of developing a mentally healthy sport organization (see Fletcher & Arnold, 2017).

Used within the context of the systems approach, the "readiness" of the sport organization can be seen in relation to human and systemic factors (Maher, 2012). These factors are likely to facilitate, limit, or otherwise curtail efforts by people—including practitioners such as you and me—in fostering mental health by means of various mental health initiatives. During my time working in a range of sport organizations, I have come to identify eight human factors important for assessing the "readiness" of a sport organization for any kind of mental health initiative (Maher, 2012). These factors, which I refer to as "organizational readiness factors," distinguish sport organizations that have the capacity to provide valuable mental health initiatives (e.g., programs and services) from those organizations unable to do so.

ORGANIZATIONAL READINESS FACTORS

This chapter will consider the eight organizational readiness factors in depth. These factors can be called the AVICTORY factors:

A – *Ability*: The extent to which a sport organization commits clearly defined resources, including personnel and funding, to mental health initiatives for its athletes, coaches, and staff.

V – *Values*: The degree to which coaches, staff, and others in the sport organization consider mental health as important and valuable to the mental and emotional development of athletes as people as well as performers.

I – *Idea*: The understanding of leaders in the sport organization regarding what athletes, coaches, and other relevant stakeholders mean by the notion of mental health.

C – *Circumstances*: The stability of the organization—in terms of structure, leadership, and staff—for addressing mental health needs of athletes and others in a meaningful way.

Figure 4.1 AVICTORY Factors

Ability
Values
Idea
Circumstances
Timing
Obligation
Resistance
Yield

T – *Timing*: The awareness among those in the sport organization concerning the most opportune time to begin working toward fostering mental health by means of programs, services, and other initiatives.

O – *Obligation*: The recognition of who in the sport organization appears to be a champion for mental health and which professionals are likely to be enthusiastic contributors to such efforts.

R – *Resistance*: The individuals or groups in or outside the sport organization who may resist a mental health emphasis for athletes, coaches, and others.

Y – *Yield*: The perceived benefits of a mentally healthy organization.

METHODS FOR ASSESSMENT OF THE ORGANIZATIONAL READINESS FACTORS

A number of methods and procedures allow us to assess the eight organizational readiness factors regarding sport organizations. The actual methods and procedures that you as a practitioner can use, however, will be determined by your role in the sport organization. The availability of information as well the willingness of people to discuss the nature and scope of the sport organization with you may also affect your use of methods and procedures.

I have found various methods and procedures productive tools for gathering organizational readiness assessment information. These methods and procedures include the questionnaire, one-on-one interview, focus group, review of written materials, and naturalistic observation. The circumstances you encounter will best determine your choice of method and procedure to use in your setting.

The *questionnaire* method is an economical one to use in gathering information about the organizational readiness of a sport organization. You can request that a range of stakeholders complete a questionnaire, thereby gaining different perspectives on the questions to which they respond. For example, you can ask athletes, coaches, athletic administrators, and parents (depending on the nature and scope of the organization) to complete and return a questionnaire pertaining to opinions and viewpoints about mental health. A limitation of the questionnaire method for assessing organization readiness for mental health initiatives is the probable need for developing more than one version of the instrument if you are going to seek responses from a range of stakeholder groups.

The *one-on-one interview* is an organizational readiness assessment method that can provide valuable and rich qualitative information about the sport organization and its readiness for mental health initiatives. However, for an effective use of the one-on-one interview method, the interviewee must meet the following conditions: (a) they must possess knowledge of the sport organization, particularly its operation; (b) they must manifest a willingness to share thoughts and opinions about mental health; and (c) they must provide accurate and valid viewpoints to the best of their abilities. Limitations of the one-on-one interview method are the time it consumes and the challenges in scheduling the interviews.

The *focus group* is a method somewhat similar to a one-on-one interview. However, the focus group method is used with a group of distinct stakeholders, such as athletes, coaches, or support staff. In a focus group, the professional leading asks the group of participants to discuss one or more questions the leader has selected in advance. For example, a leader may ask a focus group of athletic coaches how important mental health is to their athletes, how they define mental health, and what they consider important benefits of having positive mental health. A limitation of the focus group method is that one or a few individuals might dominate group conversation and therefore unduly influence discussion within the group.

The *review of written materials* is an organizational readiness assessment method that may be helpful if you can read and analyze information relating to one or more of the readiness factors. Types of written materials that could be useful to look at (if available) include program evaluation reports, organizational reports about mental health and personal development of athletes, budget and program development data, and media accounts pertaining to athlete mental health. A limitation to this method is that the information provided may be somehow biased, misleading, or incomplete.

The *naturalistic observational* method allows you to observe the operations of the sport organization. This approach is feasible when you are functioning as a practitioner or in some other related role where you have access to and substantial time with the organization. In this way, you can make judgments about organizational readiness as you interact with athletes, coaches, staff, and others. A limitation of this approach is that you may not be able to engage in enough observation of the sport organization's operations, nor may you have a sufficient period of time to complete your observations. In those cases, your observations may not represent an accurate portrayal of operations.

The remaining sections of this chapter will provide detail about the types of variables to assess for each of the eight organizational readiness factors. In reading the material in the next sections, keep in mind that you may be able to use one or more of the methods covered above.

Ability to Commit Resources to the Mental Health of Athletes and Others

A range of resources are necessary to foster the mental health of athletes and others in a sport organization. Therefore, the nature, scope, and availability of resources may very well determine what kind of mental health initiatives you or other entities (such as a mental health committee) can undertake.

The primary resource essential for mental health programming is *human resources*. These are the individuals who are ready, willing, and able to devote time and attention to mental health matters in the sport organization. These human resources may include the following:

licensed mental health professionals who can provide programs and services to athletes and others; coaches who are willing to become educated about mental health; athletic administrators who desire to support and endorse mental health initiatives; and athletes who are interested in learning how they can take care of themselves, mentally and emotionally, in relation to their mental health.

Temporal resources are another important resource. A temporal resource encompasses the amount of time that can be allotted for and dedicated to mental health initiatives in the sport organization. For instance, in order to design and implement mental health programs and services, you need time for planning, training, delivering, and monitoring these offerings. Relatedly, time needs to be available for athletes and coaches and others to attend mental health meetings and programs. Time for a focus on mental health is a resource, a valuable commodity: time must be carefully allotted and built into (already busy) schedules of athletes and others.

In addition, *physical resources* are important to the provision of mental health initiatives. Physical resources are an often-overlooked organizational commitment, yet they are significant. These resources include, but are not limited to, availability of classrooms or conference rooms for group meetings, private offices for one-on-one counseling sessions, and designated parking spaces for those involved in mental health services delivery.

Finally, and most important, *fiscal resources* are an important organizational resource. More specifically, fiscal resources include monetary funds that have been budgeted, funds that can be made available (contingent on the design of appropriate mental health programs), and compensation for mental health services providers. Without appropriate financial support, the organization will not be able to create and sustain a mental health initiative.

With respect to these organizational readiness factors—human, temporal, physical, and fiscal resources—I offer some relevant assessment questions. One or more of the assessment methods described in the prior section of this chapter can help you answer these questions.

- Has the sport organization hired or contracted licensed mental health professionals as employees or consultants? Are these professionals experienced in working with athletes and coaches?

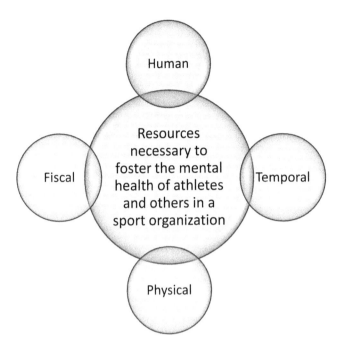

Figure 4.2 Resources Necessary for Fostering Mental Health

- Are professionals in the sport organization (other than licensed mental health providers) involved in mental health initiatives? If so, how are they involved, in light of their skills and competencies?
- Has the organization made time available for the scheduling of mental health programs and services?
- Are there facilities ready and in place where mental health programs and services can be provided?
- Are monetary funds available, or are there other possibilities for procurement of more funds for mental health initiatives?

Values and Mental Health

Values reflect the basic intentions of individuals and groups in a sport organization (Hegarty & Huelsmann, 2020). Values signify things that are meaningful and important to people, including those in a sport organization (Maher, 2011). If people value someone or something, they likely give it attention; they also make commitments to that which they perceive as having value.

Those in a sport organization may very well value the mental health of athletes, coaches, and staff. If the sport organization considers mental health a valuable, meaningful aspect of the mental and emotional development of athletes and others, then it increases the likelihood that the organization will give attention and make commitments to fostering mental health. If the sport organization does not value this task to any meaningful extent, however, then it may not prioritize, or even deem important, mental health initiatives.

The organizational readiness factor value therefore reflects how and to what extent those in the sport organization seem to value the area of mental health, based on their current understanding of it. In order to assess the extent to which the sport organization values mental health, you can seek to gather information to answer the following questions:

- Do the coaches of the various teams seem to place a value on the importance of the mental health of their athletes? What evidence, opinions, and actions indicate the degree to which coaches (individually and collectively) value mental health?
- Does it seem that athletic coaches engage in self-care regarding their own mental health and personal development?
- Have coaches involved their teams in discussions about mental health and its importance to their overall development and well-being?
- Have former athletes or other individuals been invited to speak to athletes about mental health?
- Has the sport organization made evident materials about mental health (such as posters)?

Idea of Mental Health

The idea of what mental health entails likely varies among the individuals and groups who are part of a sport organization. For instance, it is important for the practitioner to learn if athletes view mental health as being synonymous with negative terms, such as "mental case," "crazy," or "mentally incapacitated." Likewise, if the coaches see mental health as something beyond their responsibility, the practitioner needs to take those sentiments into account when educating the coaches about the nature and scope of mental health. In contrast, if the athletic administrators consider mental health as reflecting the positive mental and emotional growth of each athlete, then the practitioner can leverage this idea in their quest of fostering mental health within the sport organization.

Although it is not easy to learn how athletes, coaches, and others understand mental health, the following questions can help the practitioner obtain information about this organizational readiness factor:

- What does the idea of mental health mean to coaches of the various athletic teams? To what extent is there agreement among coaches about mental health?
- What opinions do athletes have about mental health and its meaning to them as performers and as people?
- Has mental health been a focus of staff development seminars and workshops?
- The practitioner may also ask other relevant questions about the idea of mental health depending on the size and scope of the sport organization.

Circumstances Pertaining to Mental Health

When used in the framework for the assessment of sport organization readiness for mental health initiatives, the term circumstances has a very specific meaning. "Circumstances" refers to the degree to which the sport organization is stable regarding its structure, staffing, leadership, and polices. If, for example, an athletic director or other key stakeholder who has been supportive of the mental health and total well-being of the athlete is leaving their position at the end of the year, the sport organization will be losing a very important supporter. This information is important for you, the practitioner, to know. Similarly, it would be helpful to know about circumstantial instability, such as changes in the policies of the organization that might negatively affect the development of mental health initiatives.

In order to gather information about the circumstances of the organization as they pertain to mental health, the practitioner can utilize the following assessment questions:

- To what degree will the current leadership of the sport organization support initiatives intended to foster the mental health of athletes, coaches, and staff?

- Does it appear the current leadership is likely to remain in place within the sport organization for the foreseeable future?
- Have there been recent or expected changes in the policies, purpose, and goals of the sport organization that may have implications for the organization's views on mental health?

Timing and Mental Health

Timing refers to whether and to what extent the current time is an appropriate time to begin work on the development of mental health initiatives. Within the context of any sport organization, there are times during the calendar year when the leadership prefers to begin something new or expand on an existing venture. Such times may be the beginning of an academic year, during a team's competitive off-season, or at the conclusion of the year. When considering the design and implementation of mental health programs, therefore, timing may be crucial to their success.

To glean information about the opportune time to initiate or expand a mental health venture in the sport organization, you may want to ask these questions:

- What are the typical times during the year when new programs and ventures start?
- At present, how are coaches and administrators seeming to understand mental health?
- Have there been any crises or situations in the sport organization that suggest the timing may be right to address the mental health needs of athletes and coaches?
- Other relevant, necessary questions about timing and mental health in light of the nature and scope of the sport organization.

Obligation and Mental Health

In any sport organization, there is likely at least one individual who can be considered a champion of mental health. This is a person (or people) who through words and actions has demonstrated an obligation to support and ensure that mental health takes a prominent place in the sport organization. Accordingly, it will be very useful to find out who these individuals are, what specifically they are obligated to do regarding promoting mental health, and how you may be able to support them in their efforts.

To help you learn about the obligation of individuals in the sport organization who are supportive of mental health, here are some relevant organizational readiness questions:

- What individuals or groups in the sport organization have demonstrated through words and actions that they champion mental health?
- What have these individuals done concerning the mental health domain?
- Has the organization allocated monetary funds to date for specific mental health initiatives?
- Ask any other relevant questions about the obligation factor.

Resistance and Mental Health

Despite the apparent good intentions on the part of individuals and groups supportive of a mental health perspective and emphasis in the sport organization, there are likely other individuals who will resist such efforts. These resistant individuals could be union representatives or others with vested professional or personal interests. Such people may manifest overt kinds of resistance, such as not attending meetings about mental health or ignoring communications about mental health. Relatedly, some individuals may be more covert and passive in their resistance; for instance, they may not return requests for completion of questionnaires or may abstain from a vote about moving ahead with the development of a mental health program.

To learn more about possible resistance to mental health in the sport organization, the following assessment questions may be useful:

- What individuals or groups may not be in favor of mental health initiatives? What might be their motivations?
- What evidence exists in the sport organization that suggests resistance to mental health initiatives?
- Other relevant questions about resistance.

Yield and Mental Health

Mental health programs, services, and related undertakings intend to provide benefits to athletes, coaches, and others in the sport organization. In essence, such initiatives are intended to yield benefits to those individuals and teams. Thus, it will be helpful to gain understanding about how athletes, coaches, and others perceive the benefits of mental health.

Toward that end, here are questions that can focus your assessment of this organizational readiness factor:

- What benefits do athletes perceive for themselves if they are to be involved in mental health programs?
- What do coaches consider benefits to them and to their respective team with regard to mental health initiatives?
- How do athletic administrators view the return on investment in mental health offerings in their organization?
- Other relevant questions.

UTILIZATION OF ORGANIZATIONAL READINESS ASSESSMENT INFORMATION

Once you have obtained organizational readiness assessment information about all or some of the eight organizational readiness factors, you can use that information to make some judgments about readiness. Accordingly, you can determine which factors can be considered strong points in terms of readiness (green flag), which factors are not clear and thus require additional information (amber flag), and which factors are clearly cause for concern (red flag).

Another way to utilize and consider the readiness of the sport organization for mental health initiatives is to use the *Organizational Readiness for Mental Health Checklist* (Table 4.1). In this checklist, for each of the eight factors, you make a rating of yes, no, or uncertain. Then, based on your ratings, you can identify those factors where there seems to be organizational readiness, factors where the organization does not appear to be ready, and factors where there is uncertainty due to lack of information or conflicting views. You can also note action steps needed to move from not ready or uncertain to ready.

You can the sample organizational readiness checklist of Table 4.1 to record information during your organizational readiness assessment.

Table 4.1 Organizational Readiness for Mental Health Checklist

	Yes (Ready)	No (Not Ready)	Uncertain (Unclear)	Action Steps
Ability				
Values				
Idea				
Circumstances				
Timing				
Obligation				
Resistance				
Yield				
Other comments:				

Practitioner Exercises

1. Recall one or two mental health programs you developed or in which you participated. Consider the success or lack of success of the implementation of those programs. What organizational readiness factors seemed to facilitate or limit the successful implementation of those programs?
2. What have been your experiences with the readiness of one or more sport organizations regarding mental health programs and services? What factors did you not consider then but now, in retrospect, would have been helpful to know?
3. How have you dealt with people who have resisted focus on mental health? How have you dealt with people who seemed to champion the focus? What precautions and approaches did you take with these distinct groups?

Five

This chapter provides guidelines for how to identify and gain commitments from a range of individuals who can contribute to fostering mental health and thereby assist with the development of a mentally healthy sport organization. First, the chapter offers a rationale for making mental health something for which a range of individuals in a sport organization, including athletes, are responsible. Second, it delineates an approach for identifying mental health contributors. Third, using the four Rs framework, the chapter describes the roles, requirements, responsibilities, and relationships of individuals who can contribute to mental health based on their education, training, and skill sets. Fourth, it discusses how to secure contributors' commitments to being involved in the mental health domain. Fifth, the chapter offers suggestions for how to meet with mental health contributors. Sixth, it sets forth procedures for the supervision of those who intend to contribute to mental health initiatives. Finally, the chapter concludes with practitioner exercises.

MENTAL HEALTH AS A MULTIDISCIPLINARY RESPONSIBILITY

In my professional judgment—which is shared with researchers and other practitioners—the task of fostering mental health and developing a mentally healthy sport organization is not the purview of any one individual or group of stakeholders (Henriksen et al., 2020). Rather, the task is complex: establishing the conditions for building a mentally healthy organization involves mental health initiatives and contributors at individual, team, and organizational levels.

Consequently, it is worthwhile to have as many people as possible associated with the sport organization commit to being active contributors to mental health, in light of their education, training, and skills sets and in accord with relevant ethics codes (Muir & Munroe-Chandler, 2020; Neil et al., 2017). This kind of multidisciplinary

DOI: 10.4324/9781003159018-5

collaboration is not surprising, since a range of risk and protective factors affect the mental health of athletes and others at individual, team, and organizational levels. (These risk and protective factors have been discussed in Chapter 2.)

As I have worked in professional and collegiate sport organizations over the years, it has become very apparent to me that athletes, coaches, and staff engage with one another in many discussions, daily and throughout the year. Some of these discussions—seemingly increasingly so—are related to the domains of mental performance and mental health. That is, athletes typically are inclined to talk to and listen to coaches, athletic trainers, and other staff about their psychological, emotional, and social well-being. Due to the close, daily contact with these professionals, athletes tend to discuss personal things with them, rather than with mental health professionals. For example, an athlete may confide in their athletic trainer about feeling moody, anxious, or depressed rather than talking about such matters with a licensed professional counselor (at least initially).

Since matters related to mental health and well-being affect athletes, coaches, and staff, then these individuals, in conjunction with licensed mental health professionals, can make useful contributions from their educational and training perspectives and skill sets. Subsequently, any action that assists athletes to learn more about themselves as both performers and people (over and above their sport) functions as a contribution to mental health.

Mental health contributions are valuable because ongoing efforts can help to foster the mental health of an individual, team, or sport organization. Thus, we can label any individual who, within the scope of their professional qualifications, helps athletes to be the best version of themselves as a "contributor."

Important contributors to mental health encompass many facets in a sport organization. For example, a coach expressing genuine concern for the mental and emotional needs of their athletes serves as a significant contributor, as does an athletic trainer encouraging athletes to seek mental health services. Similarly, other contributors could be a mental performance consultant listening to athletes and maintaining their confidentiality about personal matters, a professional remaining within the scope of their competencies when dealing with the mental health matters of athletes, and a sport psychologist involved in screening athletes for mental health concerns. Yet another contributor may be the coordinator of sports medicine referring athletes to appropriate licensed mental health professionals, just as a director of psychological services taking the lead on monitoring and evaluating mental health programs and services would also function as a contributor to mental health in the sport organization. Moreover, an athlete can contribute to the mental health of their peers by caring for them as people (over and above sport), by listening to them non-judgmentally, and by encouraging them to seek professional help. In short, there are many ways to contribute—or be a contributor—to a mentally healthy sport organization.

IDENTIFYING MENTAL HEALTH CONTRIBUTORS: THE 4Rs FRAMEWORK

As we have seen, a range of individuals associated with a sport organization can contribute to the mental health of athletes, teams, and the sport organization. It will be helpful, however, to utilize a way to identify such people and discern how they may contribute to the mental health domain.

Toward that end, as a practitioner, I have employed a very useful framework for assessing and determining possible contributors to mental health in a sport organization. I recommend this framework; I refer to it as the 4Rs for mental health contributors. As you consider each possible mental health contributor, you can take into account these 4Rs: Role, Requirements, Responsibilities, and Relationships.

The role the contributor in a sport organization assumes reflects what part they can play in supporting mental health in the sport organization. For example, a role of the contributor may include listening non-judgmentally to the concerns of athletes about their

Figure 5.1 4Rs Framework

personal problems and assisting them in being referred to licensed mental health providers (e.g., a mental performance coach). Likewise, contributors may take the role of assessing the mental health needs of athletes as the basis for the design and implementation of mental health programs (e.g., licensed sport psychologist). Similarly, their role may be providing direct mental health assistance to athletes (e.g., mental health clinician).

The requirements of the contributor refer to what they can contribute based on their education, training, and skill sets. For instance, as a mental health professional, a licensed sport psychologist will have education and training credentials that are different from a mental skills consultant or an athletic coach. In this regard, the requirements of the contributor will determine in large part how that professional can support mental health initiatives.

The responsibilities of the contributor relate to the kinds of actions and activities in which they can engage to support the mental health of athletes and teams. For example, the responsibilities of a licensed mental health clinician will be wider in nature and scope, technically and in terms of skill set, than that of a strength and conditioning staff member.

Finally, the relationships of the contributor reflect how they communicate with one another about athletes as well as the extent to which they can share information about mental health. This R thus includes matters of confidentiality, knowing the limits of one's professional competence, and being willing to be part of a larger mental health team or committee. For example, an athletic coach, in seeking to develop their athletes as performers and people, conveys to their athletes genuine and informal concern for their development; at the same time, they let their athletes know there are more qualified professionals to interact with them and provide them with some personal guidance.

APPLICATION OF THE 4Rs FRAMEWORK ACROSS TYPES OF CONTRIBUTORS

In any sport organization, there are many individuals who have the potential to contribute to fostering the mental health of athletes, coaches, and staff. Using the 4Rs framework described above, and based on my professional experiences as a sport and performance psychologist at the professional and collegiate levels, I have listed below some *examples* of various mental health contributors. These are people whom I have identified, and they have been committed to and successful in their respective roles in support of mental health in a sport organization.

It is important for me to note here that these examples are not exhaustive of all possibilities; indeed, I could have listed other examples, based on the sport organization and its relevant context. Nonetheless, I provide the following examples to illustrate contributors with whom I have actively worked in my role as a sport and performance psychology consultant. For each example, I employ the 4Rs framework and demonstrate how it relates to each contributor. The value of the 4Rs framework is that it is a proven approach for identifying the types of professionals associated with a sport organization who can become committed contributors to fostering mental health, in various ways, in a sport organization.

1. Sport psychologist
   a. *Role:* This professional directs the delivery of mental skills and mental health programs and services in the sport organization, typically as an employee of the organization or as a dedicated contracted consultant.
   b. *Requirements:* This professional possesses licensure as a psychologist in the jurisdiction in which they practice. They also have documented graduate education and continuing education in sport psychology in addition to overall clinical training in psychology.
   c. *Responsibilities:* This professional contributes to mental health for athletes, coaches, and staff in numerous ways. For instance, they ensure that the mental health programs and services provided to athletes and others are based on their mental health needs and are evidence-based in nature and scope; they also design and implement programs and services for athletes and others. Further, they monitor the delivery of mental health programs and services so only qualified individuals provide such services.
   d. *Relationships:* This professional serves as the supervisor of mental skills coaches and mental health clinicians while also manifesting leadership in the task of fostering athlete mental health.

2. Mental health clinician
   a. *Role:* This professional provides contracted mental health services to athletes and staff, based on referrals from a sport psychologist, other qualified professionals, or self-referral.
   b. *Requirements:* This professional is licensed as a psychologist, clinical social worker, or professional counselor. They also should possess an understanding of the sport organization context as well as have continuing education in sport psychology.
   c. *Responsibilities:* This professional contributes to mental health in a sport organization by accepting and acting on referrals of athletes, coaches, and staff. In this regard, they engage the athlete or another individual (e.g., coach) in clinical assessment related to mental health and provide appropriate intervention or treatment.
   d. *Relationships:* This professional receives referrals and communicates with the sport psychologist about the athlete or other referred individual, given ethical standards of confidentiality.

3. Mental performance coach
   a. *Role:* This professional collaborates with athletes and coaches to enhance the mental performance of athletes and teams.
   b. *Requirements:* This professional has graduate education and training in sport and performance psychology. In addition, they may also have another sport psychology credential, such as Certified Mental Performance Consultant (CMPC).
   c. *Responsibilities:* This professional contributes to mental health in a sport organization in the following ways: they design and implement mental performance plans for athletes; they provide mental skills instruction in goal setting, visualization, energy activation, and attention control; and they make referrals for mental health services to sport psychologists or other licensed mental health providers.
   d. *Relationships:* This professional collaborates with coaches so the coaches can support the mental performance of their athletes. The mental performance coach also communicates with the sport psychologist concerning athlete mental health referrals.

4. Athletic trainer
   a. *Role:* This professional takes care of the physical well-being, health, and safety of athletes.

b. *Requirements:* This professional possesses certification as an athletic trainer and possible certification in physical therapy.

c. *Responsibilities:* This professional contributes the following: they assess the physical condition of athletes; they provide physical treatment for athletic injuries; and they involve medical specialists in the overall care and treatment of athletes.

d. *Relationships:* This professional collaborates with other performance professionals—especially with sport psychologists, strength coaches, and mental performance coaches—in the overall development of athletes.

5. Athletic coach

a. *Role:* This professional provides guidance and coaching for athletes so that they can develop as performers and as people, within and outside competitive venues.

b. *Requirements:* This professional typically has education as an athletic coach, particularly experience in coaching athletes in the sport for which they are employed as a coach. They also may have degrees in physical education and other areas of human services.

c. *Responsibilities:* This professional contributes by being responsible for developing a cohesive team, instructing athletes in mental and technical skills of the sport, and supporting the total well-being of their athletes.

d. *Relationships:* This professional communicates and collaborates with sport psychologists, mental performance coaches, athletic trainers, and others in support of the mental and physical development of their athletes.

6. Athlete

a. *Role:* The individual athlete is expected to prepare for competition in a disciplined manner, perform well given their talent and skills, and be a member of an athletic team.

b. *Requirements:* The athlete is encouraged to desire to grow and develop as a performer and person.

c. *Responsibilities:* The athlete contributes to mental health in that they are expected to be a good teammate. In this sense, they provide encouragement and support to individual teammates and other athletes as these individuals deal with the challenges and demands of athletic competition.

d. *Relationships*: The athlete can listen and learn from coaches and others.

In addition to the above examples, other individuals who are part of a sport organization also can be valuable contributors to the area of mental health. These individuals include, but are not limited to, strength coaches, nutritionists, team physicians, and nurses.

SECURING THE COMMITMENT OF MENTAL HEALTH CONTRIBUTORS

By using the 4Rs framework described above, you will be able to identify individuals who have potential to be involved in various ways in fostering mental health in the sport organization. Therefore, you have the opportunity to get those individuals committed to being involved with mental health initiatives in productive ways.

The following actions highlight the process of seeking the commitment of individuals as contributors to mental health in the sport organization:

1. *Identify*: Pinpoint the individuals you would like to become contributors to mental health in the sport organization. These are people you believe can make a valuable contribution in their area of expertise; thus, you have reason to invest time and effort in gaining their commitment.

2. *Meet*: Get together, one-on-one, with each individual to discuss mental health as a multidisciplinary endeavor—with them serving as one of many contributors—in the sport organization.

3. *Discuss*: When you meet with each individual, let them know the reasons you would like them to be a contributor and what that means to you, them, and the sport organization.

4. *Understand*: Seek to learn about and discover any concerns the individual may have about the invitation for them to become a contributor.

5. *Build*: Provide positive expectations concerning how they can be of assistance as a contributor.

6. *Outline*: Offer your vision of their roles and responsibilities as a contributor.

Figure 5.2 Process for Seeking Contributors

7. *Document:* Depending on the individual and their interest, provide a written description of their roles and responsibilities as a mental health contributor.

8. *Reinforce:* Let the individual know you appreciate their interest and willingness to contribute, given their other professional demands and time availability.

9. *Acquire:* Offer additional resources to them, such as journal articles, so they can learn more about mental health.

10. *Invite:* Encourage everyone to attend meetings with all the mental health contributors so they can meet the other contributors and learn about how you are going to proceed with fostering mental health.

CONDUCTING MENTAL HEALTH CONTRIBUTOR MEETINGS

An effective way to keep mental health contributors involved and committed to fostering the mental health of athletes is to hold routinely scheduled mental health contributor meetings. The purpose of these meetings is to review how those in attendance are contributing to mental health. It also provides a context for discussing the problems they have experienced and for exploring how they can continue to communicate and collaborate with one another.

The following questions can serve as the meeting agenda for each mental health contributor meeting:

- What has been your involvement with mental health initiatives during the time since our last meeting?
- What would you like to report about your contributions since the last meeting?
- What problems or challenges are you encountering, and how are you dealing with them?
- What are areas we can work together on going forward?
- What advice and guidance can we provide to one another about our mental health involvement?

These meetings do not have to be long. Rather, they will serve their purpose when they allow contributors opportunities to communicate and collaborate with each other, regardless of meeting length.

SUPERVISION OF MENTAL HEALTH CONTRIBUTORS

It is very important for professionals involved in contributing to mental health in a sport organization to have their contributions overseen by a supervisor; such a supervisory role is key for professional functioning and ongoing professional development. In this book, "supervision" is defined as the process of overseeing the roles and responsibilities of the mental health contributors.

In particular, supervision focuses on the following areas: (a) discerning how the individual is following through with the enactment of their role, requirements, and responsibilities as a mental health contributor; (b) monitoring the extent to which they are contributing to mental health, in light of their competencies, education, and training; (c) assessing the needs of the individual contributor for additional education and guidance; (d) learning how the person is progressing as a contributor, given their roles and responsibilities; and (e) providing feedback and suggestions concerning how the contributors can continue to succeed.

Further, I recommend that the supervisor of the mental health contributors should be a licensed professional with expertise in sport psychology and possess a graduate education or continuing education in the supervision of professionals. In short, the supervisor of the contributors should be a sport psychologist or another licensed mental health professional. (A later chapter will provide more detailed discussion about evaluation and supervision pertaining to mental health programs and services.)

Practitioner Exercises

1. Consider your previous experiences in the design and implementation of mental health programs and services. In those settings, to what extent were you able to identify and involve individuals (other than licensed mental health providers) as contributors to mental health? Why was this the case?

2. How would you attempt to convince individuals who are not licensed as mental health professionals to become involved in supporting mental health in your sport organization? What would be your message to those whom you consider to have potential to contribute?
3. Examine your beliefs and philosophy about mental health in a sport organization. Where does a multidisciplinary approach fit into your work? What resistance might you encounter, and from whom?

Six

This chapter provides guidelines for the assessment of the mental and emotional development of athletes, as both performers and people, in a sport organization. Assessment of this kind should serve as a basis for designing and implementing psychological programs and services at individual, team, and organizational levels. First, this chapter offers a context and a rationale for the assessment of the mental and emotional development of athletes in a sport organization. Second, it discusses a broad definition of this kind of assessment. Third, it describes the Mental and Emotional Strengths and Needs Assessment, including the four levels of assessment. Fourth, the chapter identifies several other forms of the assessment of athletes in support of their mental and emotional development and mental health. Fifth, it considers the relevance of mental and emotional development assessment of coaches and support staffs. Practitioner exercises conclude the chapter.

CONTEXT AND RATIONALE FOR ASSESSMENT OF THE MENTAL AND EMOTIONAL DEVELOPMENT OF ATHLETES

Implementing assessment of athletes as performers and people is an important role for practitioners. Assessment is essential as a basis for fostering the mental health of athletes and for the development of a mentally healthy sport organization. For the most part, though, professional practice has not given adequate attention to the potential for multi-dimensional assessment of athletes (Henriksen et al., 2019). Too often, psychological assessment in sport organizations has been relegated to identifying athletes' mental health problems, using diagnostic perspectives coupled with narrow clinical measures. Assessment of the mental health problems of athletes is indeed important and should not be overlooked. However, it's not the best first step in getting to know the athlete in order to provide beneficial education

DOI: 10.4324/9781003159018-6

and prevention programs and services. Instead, what needs to be taken into account—initially—is the understanding of the total athlete, that is, the athlete as a performer and person. This understanding considers the athlete both within and outside competitive environments.

In this chapter, I will describe a multi-dimensional process of assessment of the mental and emotional development of athletes. This process stems from a systems approach perspective. It views the athlete in totality: that is, as a performer and person, on and off the field or court, as well as in other contexts such as school and community. Accordingly, I will define assessment as the process of gathering information about the mental and emotional strengths and needs of the athlete. By using the resultant assessment information as a basis for making decisions, you can design and implement mental skills, life skills, and mental health programs and services focused on the mental and emotional strengths and needs of athletes at individual, team, and organizational levels.

The multi-dimensional assessment process I have formulated and used in professional practice is based on several premises. These premises are the following:

- A basic purpose of a sport organization is the development of athletes across three separate yet interrelated domains: (a) the *physical domain*—strength and conditioning; (b) the *fundamental domain*—sport-specific skills; and (c) the *mental domain*—effective use of thought, emotions, and actions.

- Development of athletes in these three domains involves ensuring they become proficient at applying knowledge and skills so they can be the best version of themselves as performers and people.

- This overall development task requires purposeful instruction, coaching, and learning experiences for the athletes. These experiences are enhanced by programs and services, some of which involve athletes' mental and emotional development.

- Assessment of the athlete is an important basis for obtaining information that can be used in the physical, fundamental, and mental development of athletes, including development in support of their mental health and overall well-being.

- With regard to the mental and emotional development of the individual athlete, assessment focuses on *how* the athlete is learning to apply thoughts, emotions, and actions that will enhance them as a performer and as a person.

- Assessment information about the mental and emotional development of the athlete should be used as a basis for designing a range of mental skills, life skills, and mental health programs and services. All these programs and services are best coordinated in support of the individual athlete, the team, and the overall sport organization.

ASSESSMENT: A BASIC STEP FOR DEVELOPING
A MENTALLY HEALTHY SPORT ORGANIZATION

Assessment is an important first and basic step in fostering the mental health of athletes in a sport organization, as well as in contributing to the development of a mentally healthy sport organization. As I have advanced in my professional practice in sport and performance psychology, I have become more and more convinced that assessment of the mental and emotional development of athletes is a practical, dynamic, and proactive way of assisting athletes to grow and develop psychologically, emotionally, and socially as performers and as people.

Several reasons underscore my conviction. First, the notion of mental and emotional development signifies a positive, forward-looking, and continuous perspective for an athlete. Coaches and others who work with the athlete every day, such as athletic trainers and strength coaches, value this vantage point. In addition, mental and emotional development of the athlete involves understanding the athlete's strengths *and* areas of need as a basis for their continued development. Therefore, a perspective on mental and emotional strengths and needs assessment allows the athlete to be seen in totality as a performer and person.

Furthermore, assessment of the mental and emotional development of athletes allows for the design and implementation of a range of programs and services intended to foster their mental performance and mental health. Relatedly, within the context of a sport organization, mental and emotional development are positive terms that focus on getting better in areas of performance and personal development. Coaches, staff, and administrators of a sport organization thus find the notions of "development" and "learning" familiar terms they themselves use positively. Similarly, an athlete who is "developing" themselves, mentally and emotionally, typically

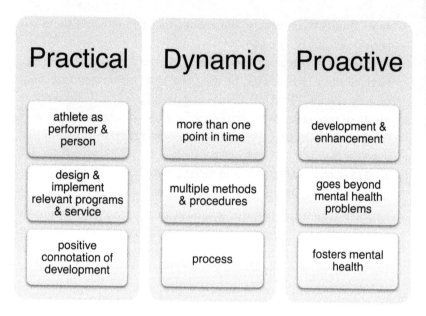

Practical	Dynamic	Proactive
athlete as performer & person	more than one point in time	development & enhancement
design & implement relevant programs & service	multiple methods & procedures	goes beyond mental health problems
positive connotation of development	process	fosters mental health

Figure 6.1 Assessment of Mental and Emotional Development of Athletes

desires to get better and improve themselves. Therefore, the practical, dynamic, and proactive way of assessment of the mental and emotional development of athletes benefits athletes psychologically, emotionally, and socially as performers and as people.

Undertaking the assessment of the mental and emotional development of athletes (and others, such as staff), however, cannot happen only once, nor is it an assessment approach relegated to one method, questionnaire, or checklist, nor focused on one diagnostic category. Rather, assessment of the mental and emotional development of athletes is best considered as a process that can take many forms, all related to mental skills, life skills, and mental health. In that regard, I have relied on various forms of assessment concerning the mental and emotional development of athletes. These, which will be discussed in more detail below, include:

- *Mental and emotional strengths and needs assessment:* This form of assessment evaluates the mental and emotional strong points and needs of the athlete as a basis for designing programs and services that will support their mental performance and mental health. This is the most basic form of mental assessment. It is intended for all athletes on a team or all the athletes who are part of a sport organization.

- *Mental health screening:* This is the process of deciding if an athlete's responses to the questions or items on a mental health screening questionnaire or checklist indicate the athlete may be at risk for mental health problems and may require additional mental assessment.
- *Mental health referral:* People typically do not consider this form of assessment a mental health assessment. However, I view it as an assessment since a mental health referral is the process of reviewing information about the athlete when there appears to be one or more mental health problems and assessing whether the athlete will benefit from a referral to a licensed mental health professional for treatment.
- *Mental health clinical evaluation:* This is the process of assessing whether an athlete requires a formal diagnosis and whether a treatment plan should be implemented for them.

A qualified mental health practitioner, either alone or in collaboration with a mental health team, oversees the task of assessing the mental and emotional development of athletes. The resulting assessment information leads to making effective decisions for athletes and others. Such decisions result in programs and services that will enhance the psychological, emotional, and social well-being of athletes.

Without a multi-dimensional approach to assessment of the mental and emotional development of athletes within the context of a sport organization, there is a likelihood assessment will be limited to a search for mental health problems and constrained by narrow assessment methods and measures. Assessment of the mental and emotional development of the athlete as a performer and person, therefore, is an important first and basic step in fostering mental health in a sport organization.

In order to proceed productively, we must define and describe what we mean by assessment of the mental and emotional development of athletes to athletes, coaches, and staff members who are part of the sport organization. Otherwise, it will be difficult to conduct meaningful information gathering with these stakeholders, since it will not be clear to them why assessment is being conducted nor what will happen with the resulting information.

The mental and emotional development assessment of an athlete involves understanding how the individual is using their thoughts, emotions, and actions as an athletic performer and person. When an athlete learns to use their thoughts, emotions, and actions effectively, their overall mental health—psychological, emotional, and social well-being—is likely enhanced.

The assessment of the mental and emotional development of athletes in a sport organization is best understood as a process. This process is an ongoing one, since information gathered about the mental and emotional development of an athlete at one point in time (e.g., beginning of the season) can change over the course of time (e.g., end of the season), based on the athlete's age, competitive experiences, and level of competition.

Typically, when the assessment of an athlete only searches for mental health problems, the focus is on whether the athlete is at risk for or qualifies as having a mental health disorder. These disorders may be ones such as depression or anxiety. Indeed, searching for mental health problems and disorders of athletes is important. However, a search for psychopathology is narrow in nature and scope. The quest often results in arriving at a psychological diagnosis, using methods intended only to assess the disorder. This approach stands in contrast to one where the focus of mental health is proactive and strengths-based, centering on the psychological, emotional, and social well-being of the athlete as a performer and person.

Qualities of the Assessment of the Mental and Emotional Development of Athletes

Unless clearly defined, the assessment of mental health of athletes in a sport organization is likely to mean different things to different people who work in that setting. To some professionals, "mental health assessment" may signify that an athlete is involved in an interview with a clinician to determine a diagnosis for a mental disorder. In contrast, other individuals may view mental health assessment as synonymous with screening athletes for mental health problems. Other stakeholders, when asked, may have no idea about what constitutes mental health assessment.

There is no uniform definition of mental health assessment of athletes in a sport organization, as far as I am aware. When the task is to enhance the mental and emotional development and well-being of athletes as performers and people, though, the practitioner's clarification of how assessment occurs serves as a very important undertaking. Without such clarification, confusion and miscommunication may result among coaches, mental health professionals, and sport administrators.

In order to proceed with the assessment of athletes regarding their mental and emotional development as performers and people, a functional definition for "mental health assessment" is valuable for understanding and for communication purposes. I have found the following definition to be very helpful in the education of athletes, coaches, and staff at professional and collegiate levels in their respective sport organizations:

- The assessment of the mental and emotional development of an athlete in a sport organization, in support of their mental performance and mental health, is an ongoing process. The process occurs under the direction of a licensed mental health professional. The purpose of the assessment is to identify the mental and emotional strengths and needs of an athlete as a performer and person. Multiple perspectives, methods, and data sources are used for assessing the athlete's mental and emotional development. The resultant assessment information can then be utilized for making decisions about designing and implementing mental skills, life skills, and mental health programs and services for athletes and others at the individual, team, and organizational levels.

When the meaning of this definition is unpacked, the following points become apparent:

1. Assessment is an ongoing process. This means that information is gathered about the athlete in a purposeful, step-by-step fashion, over the course of a season or year; it is not to be equated with testing or the interview method nor constrained to one testing session, period, or method of assessment. In this respect, the process can be considered dynamic, in that information obtained at one point in time may be collected again over the course of time.

2. The assessment process focuses on gathering information about the mental and emotional strengths and needs of the athlete as a basis for making decisions about programs and services for the athlete. In particular, learning about the mental and emotional development and overall well-being of athletes through an ongoing assessment process serves as a basis for designing mental skills, life skills, and mental health programs and services for athletes and others at individual, team, and organizational levels.

3. Mental and emotional development considers how the athlete is using their thoughts, emotions, and actions in support of their performance and personal functioning.

4. The professional who oversees the assessment process is a licensed mental health professional knowledgeable about athletes, teams, and sport organizations.

5. The information gathered as part of the assessment process allows for a more specific and richer understanding of an athlete as a performer and person.

6. Involvement in sport creates a range of demands on athletes that can affect their mental and emotional development. With the use of assessment information and with the guidance of a qualified mental health professional, the athlete can learn how to engage in the management of their thoughts, emotions, and actions in support of their overall well-being.

7. Mental and emotional assessment of athletes as performers and people is an essential part of a mentally healthy sport organization.

In light of our definition of mental health assessment, the use of multiple assessment modalities, including multiple measures and data sources, will enhance the assessment of the mental and emotional development of athletes. Thus, within the context of a sport organization, this broader conception of the process of mental health assessment allows for gathering information for decision-making about a range of program and service possibilities and at various levels of the sport organization.

MENTAL AND EMOTIONAL STRENGTHS AND NEEDS ASSESSMENT

I have formulated and implemented the mental and emotional strengths and needs assessment form of assessment over many years. I have utilized it in professional and collegiate sport organizations and continue to do so. This form of assessment reflects a practical, dynamic, and proactive process. Its intention is to learn about the mental and emotional needs of athletes, both individually and as a group. Then, using the resulting assessment information, programs and services can be designed and implemented to assist the athletes to grow and develop as performers and people, within and outside competitive environments.

This form of assessment occurs under the direction of a licensed sport psychologist or other licensed mental health practitioner, in collaboration with an athlete. Its purpose is to gather information to understand the athlete as a performer and person in areas related to the athlete's mental and emotional development and overall well-being. The information about the mental health strengths and needs of an athlete will provide you, the practitioner, with guidance about how to proceed with the athlete's mental and emotional development and well-being. You typically can employ the resultant assessment information, then, in collaboration with the athlete.

The goals of mental and emotional strengths and needs assessment are:

1. To gather information about the mental and emotional strengths and needs of the athlete as a performer and person. In this sense, "mental and emotional development" refers to how the athlete uses their thoughts, emotions, and actions, within and outside competitive venues.
2. To use the resulting assessment information to provide programs and services that will benefit the athlete as well as other athletes with similar needs. (Here, I define "need" as an area where the athlete can further develop mentally and emotionally so they can be the best performer and person possible.)
3. To monitor the mental and emotional development of the athlete at distinct points in time, such as at the beginning, mid-point, and conclusion of the season.

The mental and emotional strengths and needs assessment approach occurs in a collaborative manner between the athlete and the practitioner. At the beginning of this collaborative process, the practitioner will inform the athlete that the assessment information will be used with the athlete in assisting them to be the best version of themselves as a performer and person. Relatedly and most important, the practitioner must assure the athlete that the information generated during the assessment process is confidential and will not be shared with others without the expressed written permission of the athlete.

Mental and emotional strengths and needs assessment considers the individual athlete at four separate yet interrelated levels of mental and emotional development. Each level contributes to the mental performance, mental health, and well-being of the athlete, within and outside competitive venues and experiences. I have found that, for the most part, these four levels have made sense to the athletes engaged with me and other practitioners. The four levels—which I will discuss in more detail—are athlete as *person*, "*coper*," *teammate*, and *performer*.

At each level of assessment, the practitioner, in collaboration with the athlete, can use various methods, instruments, and procedures. It is important to note here that the assessments do not have to occur all in one day. For instance, assessment at each level can occur on separate days, given the circumstances (e.g., travel, practice schedules). Moreover, assessment may occur before, during, or after the season as a means of monitoring the mental and emotional development and well-being of the athlete.

Benefits of the Strengths and Needs Assessment

You can facilitate the following kinds of decisions based on the assessment information gained from the mental and emotional strength and needs assessment:

- Identify the mental and emotional strong points of the athlete so they can continue to develop and sustain those strengths. These strengths may include, for example, their self-understanding, perspective on sport and life, or their capacity to cope effectively with risky people, places, and things.
- Pinpoint areas of mental and emotional development in need of improvement to enhance their well-being as a performer and person. For instance, an athlete may need to learn to be more effective at balancing their sport with the rest of their life or learn to set personal goals and follow through in their pursuit.

- Specify areas of mental and emotional development of the athlete that suggest additional forms of assessment. For instance, an athlete may want to learn more about how they can be a good teammate and interact productively with coaches.
- Design and implement mental skills, life skills, and mental health programs and services that may benefit the athlete as well as other athletes.
- Monitor how the athlete is progressing regarding their mental and emotional development, over the course of time.

The strengths and needs form of assessment is appropriate to use when the following conditions exist in the sport organization:

- There is a licensed sport psychologist or another qualified licensed mental health practitioner who can oversee the assessment process.
- The practitioner and mental health team have committed to monitor the mental and emotional development of each athlete in the sport organization as a basis for building on the athlete's mental and emotional strong points and aiding in addressing identified athlete mental health needs.
- There is a professional desire to aggregate mental health needs assessment information obtained from various athletes as a basis for program development for a team or an entire sport organization.

Practitioners use a range of methods and procedures to conduct a mental and emotional needs assessment of this type. These methods and procedures include, but are not limited to, checklists and inventories, one-on-one interviews with the athlete, feedback from coaches and staff, and review of written information. As we examine the four levels in more detail, I will discuss methods that work best at each level and provide sample questions for the assessments.

FOUR LEVELS OF MENTAL AND EMOTIONAL STRENGTHS AND NEEDS ASSESSMENT

The four levels of mental and emotional strengths and needs assessment are athlete as *person*, "*coper*," *teammate*, and *performer*.

Figure 6.2 Four Levels of Mental and Emotional Development

Level 1: Assessment of the Athlete as a *Person*

The purpose of assessment of an athlete at this level of mental and emotional development is to learn how they perceive themselves as a person, over and above sport. This level focuses on how well the athlete understands both their strong points as a person and the areas they need to improve. In particular, this assessment evaluates the extent to which the athlete has clarified their *values*, has a *vision* for success, and understands their *personality*. The athlete can be involved in this assessment either by means of a one-on-one interview or a written survey. (I typically use the survey method when the strengths and needs assessment is done as part of a team or group.)

At this level, the assessment investigates the following areas:

Values: You can ask the athlete to consider their values, that is, the things that provide meaning to them in their life. In this regard, the practitioner can engage the athlete in discussing and then responding to these questions:

- What are three things that are important in your life?
- Why is each one of these things important to you?
- What does participating in sport mean to you?

- What concerns do you have about participating in sport in relation to the rest of your life?
- What would you like to improve concerning learning about and clarifying your values?

Vision: Once the athlete has responded to the questions about their values and their understanding of those values, you can engage them in discussing and responding to these questions:
- What does success as a person mean to you?
- Can you describe your vision for success?
- What factors may prevent you from making your vision of success a reality?
- What concerns do you have about being successful?
- What would you like to improve with regard to being a success?

Personality: Explain to the athlete that you would like to learn how they view their personality. Toward that end, you can ask the athlete the following:
- What is your personality, that is, the traits and dispositions that make you a distinct individual?
- What areas of your personality are your strongest?
- What areas of your personality need improvement?
- What would you like to learn more about concerning your personality?

You can review the above assessment information about the athlete's *values, vision,* and *personality* to determine areas in need of attention as well as areas that seem to be strong points for the athlete. The review can occur in collaboration with the athlete. In so doing, you can further seek to obtain the athlete's thoughts and opinions about any unclear responses. As a result of this level of assessment, you can help the athlete to identify and clarify their values, vision, and personality, both their strong points and areas of need.

Level 2: Assessment of the Athlete as a *"Coper"*

This level of assessment focuses on how well the athlete uses their thoughts, emotions, and actions to cope in an effective manner with the risks they encounter in sport and life—hence the word "coper."

The particular emphasis here is how the athlete deals with risky *people*, *places*, and *things* that could derail them; this level also asks what they need to be able to cope effectively with these risk factors.

During the assessment at this level, you can ask the athlete to respond to each of the following items below as part of a question-naire, asking them to rate their answers. This rating scale can be used for each item: 1 = doing well with this item; 2 = need to improve here; and 3 = real problem area. (It also is possible to interview the athlete regarding these items.)

- I am not easily influenced by other people who do not have my best interest at heart.
- I have difficulty recognizing people who are not good for me.
- I am able to express opinions to other people when I do not agree with them.
- I avoid the use of drugs not prescribed for me by a licensed medical practitioner.
- I avoid the use of performance-enhancing substances.
- I am able to avoid things that are not important to my well-being so I can concentrate on what is important.
- I can choose friends who are supportive of me.
- I make healthy choices about food.
- I do not worry about things that can happen to me that are not in my control.
- I avoid public and private places that put me at personal risk.
- I remain in a positive, upbeat mood most of the time.

As a related assessment task, you can ask the athlete to respond to the following questions:

- What people, places, and things can derail you (if you do not watch out for them)?
- What would you like to learn more about regarding dealing effect-ively with people, places, and things that place you at risk?

Based on the needs assessment information you obtain at this level, you can identify knowledge and skills the athlete can further develop so they can cope in an effective manner with unwanted people, places, and things.

Level 3: Assessment of the Athlete as a *Teammate*

This level considers how well the athlete uses their thoughts, emotions, and actions when interacting with other people—teammates, coaches, and staff. It also queries how the athlete accepts their *roles, responsibilities,* and *relationships* as a member of a team. The assessment of the athlete as a teammate will allow you to learn about their social functioning and how they relate to other people. To gather assessment information at this level, you can ask the athlete to rate themselves on the following questionnaire items, using this rating scale: 1 = doing well; 2 = need to improve; and 3 = real problem area for me. (Naturally, you also could ask an athlete these questions as part of a one-on-one interview.)

- I accept my role on the team.
- I respect my teammates as people, over and above their performance.
- I listen to my coaches and instructors.
- I feel that I am a member of the team.
- I can accept criticism from coaches and staff.
- I am a responsible teammate.
- I function as a leader of teammates.

Further, you can ask the athlete the following questions:

- What areas are your strongest as a teammate?
- What do you need to improve as a teammate?
- What would you like to learn more about with respect to being a good teammate?

Based on this assessment information, you will learn about areas the athlete considers their strong points as a teammate and areas in need of continued mental and emotional development.

Level 4: Assessment of the Athlete as a *Performer*

This level addresses competition and the stress that comes with being a competitive performer. Assessment involves how well the athlete uses their thoughts, emotions, and actions to *prepare* for competition, to effectively deal with the demands of competition and *compete moment to moment,* and to *evaluate* the results of their performance in a meaningful way. For this fourth level of assessment, you can ask the athlete to rate themselves on a questionnaire that addresses their mental perform- ance. This rating scale can be used for the items that appear below: 1 = doing well; 2 = need to improve; and 3 = real problem area for me.

- Balancing sport with the rest of my life.
- Understanding my strong points and limitations as an athlete.
- Setting and pursuing meaningful goals.
- Committing to plans and routines.
- Believing in my capacity to compete.
- Competing at an effective level of energy and effort.
- Paying attention to what matters at the moment.
- Remaining calm and poised under competitive pressure.
- Interacting with teammates and coaches.
- Being accountable and responsible for my performance.
- Striving to get better, even despite adversity.

In addition, you can ask the athlete the following questions:

- Which of the above areas causes you the most stress?
- Which areas would you like to learn more about?

Using the information obtained from this level of assessment, you can identify areas where the athlete excels as well as areas that require mental and emotional development and possible programming at individual, team, or organizational levels.

OTHER ASSESSMENTS

There are other kinds of assessment approaches related to mental health and important to the development of a mentally healthy sport organization. These assessment approaches have their own purpose and activities; they can serve to complement and support the quest for the mental and emotional development of athletes in a sport organization.

Screening for Mental Health Problems

We can consider mental health screening a form of mental health assessment. Mental health screening intends to gather information about an athlete, namely information that suggests the individual may be experiencing mental health problems or difficulties. For instance, you may want to screen for mental health problems that may indicate anxiety, depression, substance abuse, social phobia, disordered eating, stress, and suicide. Based on screening results, if the athlete shows signs of possible mental health problems, it may be important to have the athlete involved in additional forms of mental health assessment.

Typical screening for athlete mental health problems employs one or more screening instruments. For the most part, these instruments intend to obtain information on specific problem areas related to mental health. Here are some examples of mental health screening instruments that have technically defensible qualities for various mental health problems. I have listed them to provide a sense of the range of possibilities; their inclusion here does not mean they should be used in your sport organization, unless applicable. Details about the following screening instruments can be found in Haugen et al. (2018).

- *Anxiety:* Generalized Anxiety Disorder 7 (GAD-7).
- *Depression:* Center for Epidemiological Depression Scale Revised (CESD-R); Patient Health Questionnaire (PHQ-9P).
- *Anxiety:* Liebowitz Social Anxiety Scale (LSAS); Stanford Presenteeism Scale (SPS-6).
- *Stress:* Perceived Stress Scale (PSS).
- *Eating disorders:* Eating Disorders Test (EAT-26).
- *Attention deficit hyperactivity disorder:* Adult ADHD Self-Report Scale (ASRS); Conners' Adult ADHD Rating Scale (CAARS).
- *Substance use (alcohol):* Alcohol Use Disorders Identification Test (AUDIT).
- *Substance use (drugs):* Drug Abuse Screening Test (DAST).

Another relatively new mental health screening instrument is the IOC Sport Mental Health Assessment Tool 1 (SMHAT-1), which was developed by the International Olympic Committee (Gouttebarge et al., 2020). The SMHAT-1 consists of several sections. The first section is a mental health screening tool used for triage purposes. The second section consists of six disorder-specific screening instruments. The third section deals with a clinical assessment. A sports medicine physician or a licensed mental health professional (e.g., psychologist or psychiatrist) should use the SMHAT-1 for screening athletes.

Another screening instrument for athletes regarding their mental health is the Athlete Psychological Strain Questionnaire—APSQ (Rice et al., 2019). The ASPQ is a brief, self-reported rating scale of ten items specific to the athletic context. It is used to assess difficulties with team-based interactions, impulse control, frustration tolerance, worries, and stress (Rice et al., 2019).

We should not construe the mental health screening of athletes, though, as a straightforward endeavor. Rather, the practitioner or mental health team must give considerable thought and attention to implementing mental health screening in the sport organization. Here are guidelines that I have found helpful toward successful implementation of a mental health screening process of athletes in a sport organization:

1. Decide the purpose of the screening in the sport organization. Give specific attention to what you would like to learn through the implementation of this kind of mental health assessment approach.
2. Identify those individuals who will be responsible for and involved in the screening process. Verify they are appropriately licensed or credentialed to do so.
3. Pinpoint the athletes who will participate in the mental health screening. Know why they have been chosen as the target population for mental health screening.
4. Select the screening instrument(s) that will be used in the screening process.
5. Discuss the screening with the athletes and others, such as coaches, and explain how the results of the screening will be utilized.
6. Construct a screening protocol: who will do what, when, where, and over what time frame.
7. Clarify who will analyze and interpret the screening results.
8. Formulate a process for providing feedback to those who were involved in the screening.

Mental Health Referral

We can also consider mental health referrals a form of mental health assessment. As a mental health assessment approach, the purpose of a mental health referral is to review information available on the athlete concerning their mental and emotional development and overall mental well-being. This information may have come from various sources such as mental skills and mental health checklists that were completed by the athlete or other parties (like coaches); other sources may include interviews and discussions with the athlete, indicators about the behavior of the athlete in school or community settings, drug screen failures, and/or reports that have been generated about the athlete.

Once you, either alone or with the mental health team, review the information, you can assess whether and to what extent the athlete will benefit from being referred to a qualified mental health professional for mental health assistance (clinical assessment and treatment).

When conducting an assessment regarding a referral of the athlete to a qualified mental health professional, take these steps:

1. Make certain the assessment information on the athlete is valid and trustworthy so you are comfortable making the referral.
2. Identify the mental health professional to whom you want to refer the athlete.
3. Inform the athlete—and the athlete's parents if necessary—that you would like to make a referral, and discuss the reasons for it.
4. If the athlete and/or the parents of the athlete give permission to proceed with the referral, proceed to take that action.

Clinical Mental Health Assessment

A professional who has appropriate education and training in mental health assessment and treatment should undertake this form of mental health assessment, in light of the needs of the athlete. Typically, clinical mental health assessment involves the use of a range of methods by the clinician. These methods include the following: review of relevant medical and psychological records; psycho-social history; clinical interview with the athlete; completion of specific questionnaires by the athlete; and feedback from other significant people in the life of the athlete, such as coaches, parents, or spouse. Often, the clinician makes a clinical diagnosis based on the criteria contained in the Diagnostic and Statistical Manual of Mental Disorders (DSM-5).

If you are called to work with the coaches and staff regarding their mental health, then mental health assessment is an important—indeed necessary—first step in supporting them. I have successfully adapted and used the Mental and Emotional Strengths and Needs Assessment process I have described above (for athletes) with coaches and staff. As you make adaptations, you will need to change the wording on some of the assessment questions so the questions apply to professionals rather than athletes. However, you can employ most of the mental health screening instruments previously discussed without adaptation, except for the SMHAT-1 (since it was created only for the assessment of athletes).

Practitioner Exercises

1. Think about the forms of mental health assessment you have used in conjunction with athletes in your role as a practitioner within the context of a sport organization. Which forms of assessment were you most comfortable using, and why? Which other forms of assessment would you have liked to use, and why did you not engage in them?
2. Consider your professional experiences in providing feedback to athletes about the results of their mental health assessments. What rules and procedures have guided you in providing them with such information? How can you continue to develop and improve in the area of mental health assessment feedback?
3. How would you deal with the request of an athletic director to share the results of the mental health screening of athletes that you conducted?

Seven

This chapter provides perspectives and guidelines for the design and implementation of mental health programs and services for athletes as well as for coaches and staff. First, the chapter gives a rationale for using a program development process for designing and implementing mental health programs and services in sport organizations. Second, it offers definitions of mental health programs and mental health services in order to clarify what these terms mean and how to plan them. Third, the chapter describes a proven program development process that a practitioner as well as a mental health team can use for the design and implementation of mental health programs and services. Fourth, it sets forth a typology of mental health programs and services, illustrating the kinds of mental health programs and services that may be possible in local sport organizations for athletes, coaches, and staff. Practitioner exercises conclude the chapter.

RATIONALE FOR UTILIZATION OF A PROGRAM DEVELOPMENT PROCESS

To foster the mental health and well-being of athletes, coaches, and staff in a sport organization, you must design, implement, and evaluate programs and services in a way that provides value to these stakeholders (Maher, 2021a). Lack of attention to detail, coupled with a lack of understanding about what can constitute mental health programs or services, makes likely that such offerings will not be sustainable in a sport organization. In my professional judgment and experience, mental health programs and services in sport organizations can be considered valuable to participants and sustainable over the course of time. However, the value of such programs will be realized only if they are customized to the needs of athletes, coaches, and staff for whom they are intended, within relevant cultural and organizational contexts.

DOI: 10.4324/9781003159018-7

To achieve valuable and sustainable mental health programs and services for athletes and others in sport organizations, I recommend practitioners apply a program development process (Maher, 2021a). (The practitioner can apply this process either alone or in conjunction with a mental health team.) More specifically, this chapter covers the program development process that constitutes how the practitioner thinks about, formulates, provides, evaluates, and adjusts the mental health programs and services. By following this process, programs and services can remain in operation over the course of time, thereby contributing to a mentally healthy sport organization.

When the practitioner follows and engages in a program development process, a range of activities occur. These activities allow for programs and services that foster mental performance and mental health of athletes. These program development activities include:

- Clearly identifying the target population of athletes expected to benefit from a program or service.
- Assessing and determining the mental and emotional needs of the target population of athletes within the relevant cultural and organizational context.
- Establishing the purpose and goals of the program.
- Placing the design of the program in a form that the practitioner, in concert with other professionals, can implement and evaluate.
- Ascertaining a way to monitor the implementation of the program.
- Formulating and using a plan for the evaluation of the program.

The program development process for athlete mental health stands in contrast to an "off the shelf approach." In the "off the shelf approach," a practitioner selects an intervention to employ with athletes, often based only on material found in a journal article, book, or other document. Then, unfortunately, the intervention is used without attention given to the athletes to whom it is directed; more particularly, it ignores the athletes' specific mental and emotional needs as well as the relevant context in which those needs are embedded.

In contrast, when the practitioner applies a program development process, the athletes and their mental and emotional needs receive

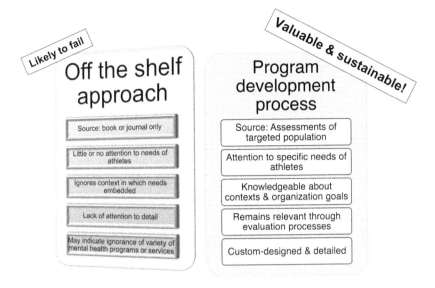

Figure 7.1 Different Approaches to Program Development

professional care and attention. A program then is custom designed for them in their sport organization. When this happens, the likelihood increases that the program or service will have value for the participants of the program regarding mental skills, life skills, and mental health. Furthermore, when the value of a program is documented—through, for instance, a record of attained goals and participants' positive reactions—the likelihood increases that the mental health program or service will be sustained over the course of time such as weeks, semesters, or years.

DEFINITIONS OF A MENTAL HEALTH PROGRAM AND A MENTAL HEALTH SERVICE

Before a practitioner can apply the program development process for the design and implementation of mental health programs and services for athletes, coaches, and staff in a sport organization, it is important to define the meaning of the terms "mental health program" and "mental health service." Otherwise, all those concerned—such as the mental health team and the coaches and staff who support the athletes, as well as perhaps the athletes themselves—will be uncertain what is being considered and planned.

A *mental health program* for implementation within the context of a sport organization is construed as a configuration of resources. These resources include the following:

- Human resources: program consultants and program implementers.
- Informational resources: purpose and goals of the program, along with program components and content.
- Technological resources: methods, techniques, and procedures that will be used with program participants.
- Physical resources: playing facilities and meeting rooms.
- Temporal resources: the amount of time available for program activities and scheduling commitments.
- Fiscal resources: a program budget and the designation of funding sources.

These programmatic resources are the basic ingredients of the program. The practitioner can organize these resources into a mental health program. The basic intention of a mental health program is that its participants—e.g., athletes—attain one or more goals that have to do with their psychological, emotional, and social well-being. In other words, we can expect that through the mental health program, the participants will develop and improve as both performers and people.

Examples of Mental Health Programs

Within this definitional context, I have listed below *examples* of what I label as mental health programs, broadly conceived. These are programs in which I have been directly involved in terms of their design, implementation, and evaluation. These program examples are wide-ranging in nature and scope. In reviewing them, though, keep in mind these are not detailed descriptions of these programs; other initiatives also are possible, depending on the nature and scope of the sport organization.

Thus, examples of actual mental health programs, based on our definition, are as follows:

- Substance use education program: This mental health program targeted athletes who were part of a large urban public high school. The program was based on the assessed needs of the athletes. The needs assessment indicated a desire by the athletes to learn about the realities and consequences of using banned drugs, performance-enhancing substances, and amphetamines.

- *Mental and emotional development coping skills program:* This mental health program involved the entire men's and women's basketball teams of a Division 1 university athletic department. The program assisted its participants in learning how to cope in an effective manner with risks encountered as student-athletes and as people, given their roles, both on campus and in the larger community. These risks included people, places, and things that could derail their performance and lives.

- *Mental skills rehabilitation program:* The participants of this mental health program were professional baseball players. These players were involved in long-term physical rehabilitation within the context of their MLB club. The purpose of the program was to help participants become skilled at taking responsibility for their physical rehabilitation by following through on it and by learning how to maintain a positive mindset (that is, managing their thoughts, emotions, and actions during their rehabilitation experiences).

- *Mindfulness development program:* This mental health program was designed for football players who were members of an NFL team. The purpose of the program was for player participants to develop their mental skills at staying in the moment as they prepared for competition. It also addressed remaining focused, play-to-play, during game competition; similarly, it taught players how to remain calm and in control emotionally off the football field.

- *Player stress management program:* The target population for this program was hockey players of an NHL team. Through the program, the players learned how to cope effectively with people, places, and things that could heighten personal stress and anxiety. In so doing, they learned how to use a cognitive-behavioral stress management process.

- *Parent mental health awareness program:* This program was designed for parents of high school student-athletes in a large suburban high school. The purpose of the program was to educate the parental participants about the demands of playing sport at the interscholastic level and about the stressful circumstances their children experienced. The program also involved guiding parental participants in understanding how to help their children balance sport with academics and other areas of their lives.

- *Mental health literacy program:* This mental health program targeted professional baseball coaches and front-office executives of an MLB club. The purpose of the program was to educate participants about mental health terms and related matters that pertained to players and themselves. Participants were trained in how they could listen and provide appropriate guidance to those players whose coaches and staff were concerned about their mental health.
- *Peer-to-peer support program:* This mental health program involved collegiate student-athletes. The program taught student-athletes how to listen and support their teammates who may be experiencing mental health problems, as well as how to encourage their teammates to seek professional assistance.

In my professional judgment, we can label all the above examples mental health programs, since each program intended to contribute to the psychological, emotional, and social well-being of those individuals who participated in them.

Examples of Mental Health Services

A *mental health service* for athletes, coaches, and staff is very similar in structure to a mental health program. Therefore, you can use a program development process in designing and implementing a mental health service. More specifically, a mental health service has to do with professionally delivered activities intended to benefit the recipient of the service. Mental health practitioners provide these activities (services) to benefit individual athletes, groups, or teams. A mental health service intends to give professional assistance related to the education, guidance, and well-being of athletes, coaches, and staff.

Below are *examples* of mental health services for athletes, coaches, and staff that qualified mental health practitioners may provide. These mental health services are like mental health programs in that they have a purpose and involve the use of specific activities. They are different from programs, however, because their utilization typically depends in part on the requests for mental health services as initiated by licensed mental health professionals.

- *Mental and emotional strengths and needs assessment:* (Chapter 6 covered this mental health service in detail.) As a mental health assessment service, the strengths and needs assessment involves professional activities in which a qualified practitioner engages. The service involves gathering information about the mental and emotional development strengths and needs of individual athletes in a sport organization as a basis for designing mental health programs.

- *Referral:* This mental health service relies on the mental and emotional needs assessment information obtained on athletes. The resulting assessment information serves as a basis for deciding if an athlete should be referred for consideration for additional mental health services.
- *Clinical intervention:* In this mental health service, a qualified practitioner applies specific methods and procedures. These methods and procedures are intended to allow the athlete to effectively manage a mental health problem such as anxiety, substance use, or depression.
- *Crisis intervention:* This service involves a practitioner or a mental health crisis team making decisions about an athlete, namely in terms of how to proceed to stabilize and support the athlete in a time of crisis.

We can call the above examples mental health services since they reflect the professional work and action engaged in by practitioners in the service of the psychological, emotional, and social well-being of athletes and others.

It is best to design and implement mental health programs and services for athletes and others by means of a program development process. In the next section, I offer an overview of the program development process I have formulated and used (Maher, 2021a). Then, in subsequent sections of this chapter, I describe each phase of the process in more detail.

OVERVIEW OF THE NATURE AND SCOPE OF THE PROGRAM DEVELOPMENT PROCESS

In order to design and implement programs and services to benefit the mental performance, mental health, and well-being of athletes and others in a sport organization, I recommend a programmatic approach to those tasks. This kind of approach is referred to as the program development process. I have applied this process over the years, routinely and successfully, with most of my sport psychology programs (Maher, 2021a).

The program development process consists of seven separate yet interrelated professional actions. The application of these professional actions by a practitioner intends to make sure the mental health program or service to be designed and implemented is customized to the mental and emotional development needs of the participants of the program, within the cultural, ethnic, linguistic, and organizational contexts in which those needs are embedded.

The program development actions you should take to create a valuable and sustainable mental health program are the following:

1. Identify and learn about the program participants.
2. Conduct a mental and emotional development needs assessment of program participants.
3. Determine the readiness of the sport organization for a mental health program.
4. Establish the purpose and goals of the mental health program.
5. Organize and formulate an evaluable mental health program design.
6. Facilitate and monitor mental health program implementation.
7. Evaluate the mental health program.

Identify and Learn about the Participants of the Program

If a mental health program is to have value for athletes, coaches, or staff—and, if interest exists, to be sustained over the course of time in a sport organization—then it is necessary to identify the program's likely participants and learn about them as performers and people. Identification of program participants means knowing the names and related characteristics of these individuals, particularly their age, gender preference, prior performance history, and number of years in competitive sports. Learning about program participants also involves understanding their culture and ethnicity and becoming familiar with any of their prior experiences with sport psychology services and mental health programs.

Figure 7.2 Program Development Actions

Table 7.1 Program Participant Survey

Chronological age	
Gender preference	
Year or level in school	
Sport(s) in which you compete	
Number of years in competitive sport	
Recent performance history	
Ethnicity	
Other relevant information	

You can obtain this kind of information by formulating a separate survey instrument or including it as part of a needs assessment (discussed in the next section). Table 7.1 is a table you could use to help you learn about the individuals who will be participating in the mental health program.

Conduct a Mental and Emotional Needs Assessment of Program Participants

In the program development process, a needs assessment serves as a means of gathering information about the mental and emotional development needs of the athletes who are going to participate in the program. You can then use this information as a basis for designing a mental health program for those athletes. Although Chapter 6 described the notion of mental and emotional development needs assessment in detail, I provide a short example here of items that can be part of the needs assessment. In the assessment, you can ask each athlete to rate themselves on specific items related to their mental and emotional development. For example, your needs assessment may look like Table 7.2.

In addition to asking the athletes about areas they need to develop, you can query coaches and others who know the athletes, such as athletic trainers, for their opinions. Toward that end, here are two questions to which these professionals can respond:

- What areas of mental and emotional development might athletes benefit from learning more about?
- What mental skills will allow athletes to enhance their psychological, emotional, and social well-being (that is, if the athletes become increasingly skilled at them)?

Table 7.2 Needs Assessment

Needs Assessment Areas			
Please rate yourself on the following items, using this scale: 1 = have a good understanding; 2 = need to learn more; 3 = problem area			
	1	**2**	**3**
Balancing sport with the rest of my life			
Being motivated to pursue meaningful goals			
Following through with plans and routines			
Having a positive outlook on things			
Being able to focus on things that are important			
Remaining calm and composed			
Handling failure effectively			
Interacting productively with others			
Not worrying about things			

Determine the Readiness of the Sport Organization for a Mental Health Program

Sport psychology programs in sport organizations do not exist in a contextual vacuum, and mental health programs for athletes are not an exception to this reality (Maher, 2021a; Wagstaff, 2017). In order for you to design and implement a mental health program successfully, the stakeholders of the sport organization must be ready for such endeavors. By determining the readiness of the sport organization for a mental health program, you will have a good idea about what may be possible in your quest to design and implement one or more mental health programs or services.

One way to determine the readiness of a sport organization for a mental health program is to consider the organization in relation to several organizational readiness factors. I have used these factors to make sense of whether and to what extent a sport organization at professional, collegiate, and secondary school levels is ready to engage in the program development process. These organizational readiness factors are as follows:

- *Ability:* The extent to which the sport organization is able to commit resources to a mental health program. These resources include program developers and staff, funding for the endeavor, facilities, and time allotments.

- *Values:* The degree to which coaches, staff, and administrators of the sport organization seem to value the mental health of athletes and are willing to engage in program development activities.
- *Idea:* Clarity regarding what the idea "fostering mental health" means to athletes, coaches, and administrators. This involves the extent to which these stakeholders view mental health as an important part of the sport organization or see mental health as a marginal matter.
- *Obligation:* The degree to which stakeholders in the sport organization are willing to work to assure the design and implementation of a mental health program for athletes. This may be manifested by attendance of stakeholders at meetings that have to do with mental health as well as by the willingness of individuals to be members of committees or working groups focused on developing a mentally healthy sport organization.
- *Resistance:* The extent to which individuals or groups associated with the sport organization may resist mental health programming efforts. Resistance may be overt (such as stating that there is no money in the budget for mental health programs) or more covert in nature (such as not providing information about their viewpoints on mental health in sport).

You can gather organizational readiness information about these factors from discussions with coaches, staff, and administrators. In addition, your own observations and informal contacts with people in the sport organization can help you obtain organizational readiness information.

Establish the Purpose and Goals of the Mental Health Program

In order for a mental health program to benefit athletes who are part of a sport organization, you need to firmly and clearly establish the purpose and goals of the program. Otherwise, the program design will not have a clear direction, and it will not be evident to coaches and others in the organization how the program benefits the participants.

The purpose statement of a mental health program is a statement that provides an initial direction for program development. A statement of program purpose offers information about the who, how, and what of the program. For example, it shows who the athletes are who will participate in the program; it also describes how the athletes will be involved in the program in terms of methods, procedures, and activities. Likewise, the statement makes clear what benefits the athletes can expect to accrue as a result of their program participation.

Here is an example of a statement of purpose for a substance use education program for collegiate student-athletes:

- All members of the men's and women's basketball teams will be involved in five weekly meetings about the use and abuse of banned substances so that they will understand and be appreciative of the risks encountered in using such substances as well as the consequences of such use.

You should base the goals of a mental health program on one or more mental health needs of the athletes who will participate in the program. The program's goals also should align with the program's statement of purpose. Accordingly, it is best to state the goals of the mental health program by describing specific knowledge, skills, or abilities that athletes will acquire based on their participation in the program.

The following are examples of two goals for a mental performance program for Major League Baseball players:

- Participants will understand the importance of acceptance in dealing with the day-to-day demands of competition at the major league level.
- Participants will be able to remain composed when facing pressure-filled game situations as each game proceeds.

Organize and Formulate an Evaluable Mental Health Program Design

For a mental health program to realize its purpose and goals for athletes, the program needs to be organized so those outcomes will occur. This kind of organization is manifested in the form of a program design. Relatedly, in order for the practitioner to make judgments about the value of the mental health program following its implementation, the program needs to be in a form that can be evaluated.

We can consider a mental health program "organized" if these conditions are met:

- The methods and activities of the program have been sequenced and linked to the program's goals.
- You have identified and trained (as necessary) the individuals who will implement the program, and they are ready for program implementation.
- The schedule of program sessions has been determined, along with meeting locations and facilities.

Once the practitioner has organized the mental health program in terms of its program design, the task then becomes making certain the program design is in evaluable form—that is, organized in such a way that it can be evaluated. An "evaluable mental health program design" means these elements are in place:

- The practitioner has established and documented the purpose and goals of the mental health program.
- The organization of the program is clear as to what methods, procedures, and activities will be implemented, as well as the when, where, and by whom.
- The practitioner has delineated program evaluation questions, along with methods and procedures to answer them, to make the following determinations:

  - *Who participated in the program?* An answer to this program evaluation question documents that the appropriate athletes participated in the program.
  - *How was the program implemented?* An answer to this program evaluation question provides information about the extent to which the program was implemented in terms of its methods, procedures, and activities.
  - *What was the value of the program?* An answer to this program evaluation question allows evaluators to make judgments about how valuable the program was to its participants and the sport organization. ("Value" has to do with the extent to which mental health program goals have been attained and how the program

benefitted the athletes, based on their reactions to the program and the degree to which they applied what they learned during the program.)

Facilitate and Monitor Mental Health Program Implementation

Once you have organized the mental health program into an evaluable program design, the program is ready to be implemented. Therefore, it is worth the time and effort to facilitate the implementation of the program as well as to monitor how the program is being implemented.

Facilitation of the implementation of a mental health program involves several controllable activities on the part of the practitioner. These activities include:

- *Discuss* the program's purpose, goals, and activities with the athletes and others who will be involved in the program, such as coaches and support staff.
- *Understand* and respond to questions, comments, and concerns these stakeholders may have about the design or implementation of the program.
- *Reinforce* the athletes, coaches, and others for their willingness to participate in the program.
- *Acquire* necessary resources so the program can be implemented on time and in accord with the design of the program.
- *Build* positive expectations about the program and the benefits to its participants (athletes) in terms of their mental performance and mental health.

As the mental health program is being implemented, take time to monitor it so you will obtain this information:

- Whether athletes are attending and participating in the program.
- The extent to which the goals of the program are being addressed through the appropriate methods, procedures, and activities.
- Whether the athletes are responding in an expected way to the program.
- Whether there is a need to make adjustments in the way the program is being implemented and is occurring.

If you (and others) have put thought, time, and effort into designing and implementing a mental health program in a sport organization, then it is important to evaluate the program in order to find out how valuable the program has been for participants' mental health and mental health needs. In this regard, you can determine the value of a mental health program using the following indicators:

- The extent to which the athletes have made progress or attained the educational or skills goals that were part of the program design.
- The reactions of athletes and other key stakeholders (such as coaches and athletic directors) to the program.
- Whether and to what extent the program can be further developed and improved.

The evaluation of a mental health program should proceed from a program evaluation plan. It is best to formulate this kind of plan when you are designing the program. In this way, program evaluation is built into the design of the program. The mental health program evaluation plan should include information about the following elements:

1. *Participant overview:* Listing of the athletes or other target population expected to participate in the program. *Who participated in the program?*
2. *Description of the program design* (so that it is clear to stakeholders about the design of the program): Who it was provided for, how it was implemented, and what it was supposed to accomplish. *What was the program that was expected to be implemented?*
3. *Evaluation of the implementation of the program:* Documenting how the program occurred according to the design of the program as well any adjustments made to it following implementation. *How was the program actually implemented?*
4. *Evaluation of the attainment of program goals:* Providing information about how the educational goals and skill goals of the program were attained. *To what extent were program goals attained?*
5. *Evaluation of reactions to the program:* Obtaining information about what athletes thought about the program as well as obtaining similar information from coaches and other key stakeholders. *How did those who were involved with the program react to it?*

6. *Evaluation of program strong points and developmental needs:* Areas of the program that need further development and improvement as well as areas that were considered solid features of it. *What were the strong points and developmental needs of the program?*

Chapter 12 will describe in detail methods and procedures to use in the evaluation of a mental health program.

TYPOLOGY OF MENTAL HEALTH PROGRAMS AND SERVICES FOR ATHLETES IN SPORT ORGANIZATIONS

There are many possible mental health programs and services practitioners can design and implement using the program development process. In this section, I provide a typology of mental health programs and services that are possible to use with athletes, coaches, and staff regarding their mental health needs.

I use the term "typology" to refer to types or categories of mental health programs and services that have potential for use in sport organizations. Exactly what programs and services may be possible will depend on several factors. These include the mental health needs of athletes, the relevant context in which those needs are embedded, and the readiness of the sport organization to support such programs.

This typology is organized by several programmatic categories. I present this information so you can see the range of possibilities. You can consider these possibilities when thinking about how to best serve the needs of athletes, coaches, and staff in the sport organization where you practice.

Below, I will describe various types of mental health programs and services—with some actual examples in which I have been involved as a practitioner. I have found these categories valuable as a basis for consideration in my work at professional, collegiate, and secondary school levels. This mental health program typology includes the following programs and services:

- Mental health screening programs.
- Mental health referral of athletes to qualified practitioners.
- Educational programs for athletes to inform them about the parameters of mental health.

- Skill-based programs for athletes that instruct them how to cope with the demands of sport and life that influence mental health.
- Mental health treatment interventions.
- Mental health programs for coaches and staff.

We will now look at each type of program or service in more detail.

Mental Health Screening Programs

Chapter 6 on mental health assessment described mental health screening in detail, so I will not detail this kind of program here. Rather, below, I highlight how you can think about mental health screening as a program.

When mental health screening is conceived of as a program, several things become readily apparent, such as the following:

1. The *target population* for mental health screening information is those practitioners who can use the screening information to learn about the athletes screened. Although the ultimate beneficiary of mental health screening program information is the athletes, the users of the information are qualified, licensed mental health professionals.
2. The *mental health needs* addressed by a mental health screening program involve reliable and trustworthy information about areas of mental health that may be problematic for the athlete and areas that may require additional assessment.
3. The *purpose* of a mental health screening program is for qualified practitioners to make decisions about how to proceed to support athletes who have participated in the screening based on the resultant information from the assessment activities.
4. The *design* of a mental health screening program should reflect the sequence and timing of screening activities, including the screening instrument and the qualifications of those involved in the screening process.

Mental Health Referral

Typically, people do not view referral of an athlete as a program but, rather, as a means of sending the athlete to a mental health provider for professional assistance. When mental health referral is framed as a program, however, the following becomes apparent:

1. The *target population* for mental health referral is the athletes whom the practitioner or mental health team considers candidates for a referral to another qualified practitioner for professional assistance.
2. The *needs* addressed by a mental health referral program reflect an understanding of the athlete in terms of their mental health; it also signifies a decision whether the athlete will benefit from additional professional assistance vis-à-vis a referral.
3. The *purpose* of the mental health referral program is to communicate and collaborate about the mental health of the athlete before proceeding to make a referral for their benefit.
4. The *design* of the mental health referral program should reflect (a) which steps are necessary to review mental health information about the athlete; (b) how it will be discussed if it is in the best interest of the athlete to receive professional assistance over and above what is possible with current professionals; (c) who are appropriate referral sources; and (d) how and when the referral decision will be made.

Educational Programs to Inform Athletes about Mental Health

Educational programs are ones that address the information needs of the mental health of athletes. Educational programs of this nature and scope intend to inform athletes about mental health—to educate them—rather than teach them specific skills. Typically, these programs occur as part of larger athlete orientation programs.

The purpose of educational programs for athletes is to provide information related to athlete mental health that will enhance their understanding. In light of this definition of educational programs for athlete mental health, I offer the following examples of educational programs that I have been involved in designing and implementing:

- An educational program that targeted college-level student-athletes to inform them about policies, procedures, and consequences related to the use of banned substances and performance-enhancing substances. This program intended to increase their self-understanding and make them aware of mental health resources they could access as student-athletes.
- An educational program for professional baseball players of a Major League Baseball organization. This program intended to enhance

Designing and Implementing Mental Health Programs and Services player awareness about domestic violence by informing them of the parameters of that term, explaining how they could identify situations that may put themselves and others at risk for violent behaviors, and discussing who to contact if they suspect domestic violence.

- An educational program for secondary school student-athletes to inform them about the use and abuse of alcohol and drugs and the consequences of using such substances.
- An educational program for rookie players of a National Football League team to educate them about mental and emotional development in addition to the resources in the organization to support them in that regard.
- An educational program for collegiate student-athletes to educate them about the area of sport psychology.
- An educational program to teach young Latin American players of a Major League Baseball organization what to expect as they transition from their cultures to the United States.

Skill-Based Programs to Support the Mental Health of Athletes

In contrast to educational programs that focus on providing information to athletes about mental health, skill-based programs intend to teach athletes specific skills that can contribute to positive mental health. Accordingly, skill-based programs involve the following elements: (a) providing information to the athletes about the skills to be learned; (b) teaching the skills to them; (c) providing opportunities to apply the skills in sport-related and non-sport settings; and (d) monitoring the progress being made with the development and maintenance of the skills.

Below are descriptions of skill-based programs intended to foster positive mental health of athletes; each program reflects the above elements. (I have been involved in the development of these programs using the process described in the prior section of this chapter.) Examples of skill-based programs include:

- A program designed to teach professional basketball players of a Women's National Basketball Association franchise how to cope effectively with people, places, and things they encounter as they progress as a professional player.

- A program designed to teach minor league players of a Major League Baseball club how to use skills to manage stressors they encounter on and off the field.
- A program designed to instruct collegiate student-athletes who are undergoing long-term physical rehabilitation how to manage the fear, worry, and doubt that can accompany their physical rehabilitation.
- A program designed to teach elite athletes of a sport academy how to be resilient in the face of adversity, particularly adversity they encounter while playing their sport, and how to be resilient in seeking to balance sport with the rest of their lives.
- A program designed to teach student-athletes from several sports how to use the Mindfulness Acceptance Commitment Approach.

Mental Health Clinical Interventions

Still another type of mental health program and service is the mental health clinical intervention. Typically, when discussion occurs about the mental health of athletes, the type of program that comes to mind for most practitioners is the mental health clinical intervention. These interventions are provided once a qualified practitioner has assessed an athlete and found an apparent mental health problem.

It is not the purpose of this chapter to offer a review of mental health clinical interventions that can be provided to athletes based on their mental health problem or diagnosis. Rather, I would like to list the mental health problem areas prevalent in athletes, typically at collegiate and professional levels, as well as suggested interventions. In this regard, mental health clinical interventions often involve these problem areas and interventions:

- *Anxiety:* Assisting the athlete to deal with the self-management of fear, worry, and doubt.
- *Depression:* Guiding the athlete to learn how to understand themselves and manage their mood, thoughts, and emotions.
- *Substance use:* Helping the athlete to deal effectively with thoughts, emotions, and actions that relate to the use and abuse of substances, particularly alcohol, drugs of abuse, and performance-enhancing substances.
- *Attention deficit hyperactivity:* Assisting the athlete to learn how to manage their attention and concentration, especially regarding listening to

coaches, instructors, and teachers, and how to recognize and deal with impulsive actions.

- *Disordered eating:* Guiding the athlete to understand their self-understanding and self-esteem as well as how to deal with food and their response to it.
- *Anger:* Instructing the athlete how to manage their anger and related emotions.
- *Sleep:* Assessing and determining an appropriate plan for managing and moderating the athlete's sleep.

Practitioner Exercises

1. What kinds of programs will be valuable to support the mental health of athletes in the sport organizations in which you work? Either alone or in collaboration with others, identify those program possibilities. Decide which one or two programs are likely candidates to develop in specific settings with some of your athletes.
2. An athletic director and a director of sports medicine ask you to develop a mental health program for student-athletes at their university. Describe how would you assist them in designing and implementing a program.
3. In the sport organizations in which you have worked or observed, what obstacles have you encountered that have prevented mental health programs for athletes from being established? For each factor that you identify, pinpoint actions you might take to remove or otherwise limit these obstacles.
4. If you had the opportunity to propose one kind of mental health program for athletes in a sport organization, what would the program be, and why?
5. What do you need to improve regarding designing and implementing mental health programs in sport organizations? How will you proceed to do so?

Eight

This chapter discusses how to involve coaches, athletic trainers, and other staff members in developing knowledge and skills so they can contribute to fostering the mental health of athletes within the context of a sport organization. First, it provides a rationale for why coaches and staff should be contributors to the mental health of their athletes, including why such involvement is necessary when developing a mentally healthy sport organization. Second, the chapter considers the ethical importance of establishing professional boundaries when educating and training coaches and staff as contributors to mental health. Third, it covers guidelines and goals pertaining to educating and training coaches and staff as contributors in support of the mental health of their athletes and teams. Fourth, it offers several overview descriptions of programs that were designed and implemented to educate and train coaches and staff about mental health in their roles as mental health contributors. The chapter concludes with practitioner exercises.

RATIONALE FOR EDUCATING AND TRAINING COACHES AND STAFF AS MENTAL HEALTH CONTRIBUTORS

Those responsible for leading and managing sport organizations make a meaningful investment when they choose to foster the mental health of athletes, coaches, and staff. This investment is meaningful and important because fostering the mental health of athletes involves many people, in diverse roles, across various sport organizational levels (Breslin et al., 2017). When the organizational leaders and managers develop a mentally healthy sport organization, coaches and staff are significant—indeed essential—contributors.

Educating and training coaches and staff as mental health contributors is important since fostering mental health in a sport organization is a multidisciplinary task. It is not relegated only to

DOI: 10.4324/9781003159018-8

those who are licensed mental health providers. Thus, those who are not licensed as mental health providers still can be valuable contributors to athlete mental health, if they are educated and trained in an appropriate manner about the mental health of athletes (Paquette & Trudel, 2018).

A sport organizational investment in fostering the mental health of athletes necessitates that coaches and other staff members engage in important functions in areas of athlete mental health. Thus, these professionals are very much mental health contributors: they are on the front line daily with their athletes. Typically, they have a very good sense of the moods, frustrations, and personal challenges their athletes are experiencing within and outside competitive venues.

Head coaches and assistant coaches are involved in many functions and activities with their athletes, both at individual and team levels. In addition to practice and game preparation and follow-through, coaches are involved in the development of their players. An important part of this development is the mental and emotional development of their athletes.

Athletic trainers are professionals to whom athletes talk about their mental and emotional needs and concerns, perhaps more so than any others who work in sport organizations. This is the case since athletes depend on athletic trainers to monitor their physical well-being and engage them in daily routines, regimens, and treatments that support the health of the total individual.

Strength and conditioning staff, too, interact formally and informally with athletes, typically daily. Although the strength and conditioning staff focus on helping athletes develop and improve cardiovascular fitness and muscular strength, these professionals also deal with the mental and emotional well-being of athletes. Often, athletes will discuss with the strength coach how they feel about things they are experiencing in their lives and share other thoughts, emotions, and actions (Gonzalez et al., 2005).

Likewise, coaches and other staff often ask *mental performance consultants and mental skills coaches* how to proceed with athletes who are not performing well and to help identify athletes who may be experiencing mental health problems. For the most part, though, mental performance consultants and mental skills coaches are not licensed to conduct mental health assessments and mental health treatment activities. Accordingly, you should expect these professionals to communicate and collaborate with licensed mental health providers about the mental health and well-being of the athletes with whom they are working.

Indeed, *all* the professionals who work in sport organizations—coaches, staff, and even administrators—can benefit from learning how they can contribute to the mental health of athletes (Duffy et al., 2019). This kind of learning can occur within their roles, responsibilities, and skill sets. When coaches and others are educated and trained about the mental health of athletes, these professionals become key people in supporting the athletes with whom they interact, since the professionals can help facilitate even more effectively the athletes' overall well-being.

ESTABLISHING BOUNDARIES FOR EDUCATING AND TRAINING COACHES AND STAFF ABOUT MENTAL HEALTH

There is increasing interest in educating coaches and others in sport organizations about mental health. Within sport organizations, "mental health literacy" has been a frequently used term, along with "mental health first aid" (Li et al., 2014; National Council for Behavioral Health, 2015). Mental health literacy has been used to signify that people from all walks of life and industries can become knowledgeable about mental health. Subsequently, the term mental health first aid also has become an increasingly prominent term related to rendering assistance in mental health, especially for non-licensed professionals.

Research about mental health literacy has been growing, too (National Council for Behavioral Health, 2015). For example, one such effort was an evaluation of a mental health literacy program in a sport organization in Australia. This program was intended to enhance the confidence of coaches about mental health by increasing their knowledge of that area (Sebbens et al., 2016). The rising attention to these topics underscores their growing importance in our field.

I support mental health literacy and mental health first aid efforts in sport as well as in other areas of performance and business. Accordingly, in my professional experience in sport organizations, I have come to rely on a broader conception than is conveyed by the term "mental health literacy." Though it often narrowly refers to learning about mental health, I consider the task broadly: mental health literacy is functionally the education and training of coaches and staff so they can communicate and collaborate about mental health with their athletes and professionals—that is, so they can be in position to provide mental health first aid. Through meaningful communication and collaboration, and with the intent of fostering the mental health of athletes as individuals and team members, coaches and staff can put themselves in a very good position to be mental health contributors.

When we analyze and utilize this broad-based conception for education and training of coaches and staff in mental health, we make possible the following contributions by coaches and staff in support of athlete mental health:

- Coaches and staff can contribute to the mental health of athletes through the following: (a) their understanding of the parameters of mental health in relation to their athletes; (b) their ability to listen attentively and compassionately to the concerns their athletes express; and (c) their working with mental health professionals so their athletes receive the mental health services they need.
- The education of coaches and staff about the mental health of their athletes also can result in the following benefits: (a) it provides coaches and staff with information about what mental health is and what it is not; (b) it helps them make distinctions between mental health inquiries, concerns, and problems of their athletes; and (c) it increases their familiarity with policies, procedures, and referral sources regarding mental health for their athletes. In this way, coaches and staff can communicate in a timely and appropriate manner with mental health professionals and other relevant stakeholders.
- The training of coaches and staff about athlete mental health involves instructing these contributors so that they can (a) become skilled at understanding their athletes as people as well as performers; (b) interact in a caring manner with their athletes concerning personal development and well-being; (c) manifest a sincere interest so their athletes will want to reach out to them for advice about mental health resources; and (d) build a team environment

conducive to mental health. Coaches and staff then can collaborate with mental health professionals and others in support of athlete mental health.

In the next sections of this chapter, I provide guidelines as well as content you can use as a basis for the design of programs for the *education and training* of coaches, staff, and administrators of a sport organization as mental health contributors. I have relied on these guidelines and content for education and training purposes as part of my professional practice in sport and performance psychology.

EDUCATIONAL GUIDELINES

The purpose of educating coaches and staff about athlete mental health is to equip them with perspectives and knowledge about the nature and scope of mental health in relation to their athletes. Such perspectives and knowledge will help coaches and staff in their professional relationships with their athletes. You can realize this type of mental health education for coaches and staff by conducting one or more educational sessions with them, perhaps as part of an overall program. As a result of their participation in such sessions, coaches and staff will be educated in ways that allow them to contribute to the mental health of the athletes in their charge.

With this purpose in mind, the following *educational goals* for coaches and staff regarding mental health are relevant:

1. Develop an understanding about the meaning of mental health as it relates to their athletes.
2. Recognize mental health situations involving their athletes and know their responsibilities so they can provide appropriate support.
3. Understand their sport organization's policies and procedures about mental health.

The best methods and procedures to attain these educational goals are group meetings, which involve presentation of information related to each goal. Following the presentation, you can facilitate a discussion of the information that was presented, including exploring how the material applies to them as mental health contributors.

Educational Goal 1: Understanding the Meaning of Mental Health for their Athletes

In order for coaches and staff to learn to function as contributors to the mental health of their athletes, an important first step is to educate them to understand mental health. That is, they need to know how to meaningfully define the mental health of their athletes. Here, I suggest the following definition to use for this kind of discussion. In essence, this is the definition of mental health on which this book is based:

- The mental health of each of your athletes reflects each individual's psychological, emotional, and social well-being. This well-being can be seen in how each athlete (a) copes with the daily demands of the day, both as an athlete and as a person; (b) follows through on their roles and responsibilities; and (c) interacts with other athletes, yourself, and staff.

You can discuss this definition of mental health with coaches and staff who are part of an educational session. In so doing, you can also request that they consider various questions and answers. Relatedly, you can mention that they should not equate mental health of an athlete solely with an absence of mental illness.

Using the above definition of athlete mental health, review and discuss with coaches and staff the following positive mental health indicators related to athletes:

- Perspective: The athlete can balance the demands associated with practices and games with other responsibilities that are not part of their athletic development or team functioning (e.g., family contacts, academic studies).
- Coping: The athlete can cope in an effective way with their performance and their overall participation in their sport. This includes coping effectively with such things as variability in performance, demands of travel, and adverse situations that arise, as well as interacting with teammates and others.
- Competitive mindset: The athlete has a mindset that is positive and allows them to prepare and perform in an upbeat and competitive manner and, in that same mindset, deal with their results.

Educational Goal 2: Understanding Types of Mental Health Situations and Responsibilities

Coaches and staff members can benefit from education about various situations their athletes may experience regarding mental health. These situations differ based on the extent to which the athletes are personally involved with matters pertaining to their mental health:

- *Mental health inquiry:* In this situation, an athlete just wants to learn more about mental health. The athlete may have been reading about mental health in sport and wants to learn what constitutes mental health. In particular, the athlete wants to learn more about mental health conditions such as anxiety, depression, or eating disorders. (Here, it is the responsibility of the coach or staff member to encourage the athlete to approach someone in the organization with expertise about mental health, such as a sport psychologist, or to find another licensed professional with whom they can engage in an informed discussion.)

- *Mental health concern:* In this situation, an athlete believes their mental health is not what it should be—according to them. The athlete may express a concern to a coach or staff member that things are not right with them, mentally, emotionally, or socially. However, despite their concern, the athlete does not want to speak with a mental health professional, at least not at the current time. In essence, the athlete is thinking about communicating and engaging with a mental health professional, but the athlete is not yet ready to do so.

- *Mental health problem:* In this situation, the athlete thinks they are experiencing a problem related to their mental health. They have expressed a desire to speak with a mental health professional; they seek the opinion of a coach or staff member about how to proceed and to find out to whom they can reach out for assistance.

- *Mental health referral:* In this situation, the sport organization's mental health team or a licensed mental health professional has referred the athlete to an outside mental health provider for mental health assessment and treatment.

- *Mental health crisis:* In this situation, an athlete needs immediate mental health assistance. Although the situation is not life-threating, the next step for the care and support of the athlete rests with the mental health team or the sport organization's mental health professional.
- *Mental health emergency:* In this situation, the athlete's mental health is considered life-threatening to the athlete and requires immediate emergency response (e.g., 911 call) by mental health professionals associated with the sport organization.

Table 8.1 Types of Mental Health Situations and Responsibilities

	Definition	Action
Mental health inquiry	Athlete wants to learn more.	Encourage athlete to seek expert.
Mental health concern	Athlete concerned for their mental health but reluctant for professional help.	Listen. Encourage athlete to seek professional help.
Mental health problem	Athlete suspects problem and asks for help finding assistance.	Refer them to appropriate mental health professionals.
Mental health referral	Mental health professional refers athlete for mental health assessment and treatment.	Check in to see that athlete has followed through with referral.
Mental health crisis	Athlete needs immediate assistance (but not life-threatening).	Mental health team or sport organization mental health professional takes charge.
Mental health emergency	Athlete's mental health is life-threatening.	Call 911.

Educational Goal 3: Understanding the Sport Organization's Mental Health Policies and Procedures

This educational goal is a basic one. You can usefully address this goal with coaches and staff in a straightforward manner, as part of an educational meeting with them. At this kind of meeting, you should discuss a range of topics, coupled with opportunities for coaches and staff to raise questions and concerns they may have.

These topics would include, but not be limited to, the following:

1. The sport organization's definition of mental health.
2. The commitment of the sport organization to the mental health of athletes and others.
3. The roles and responsibilities of the sport organization's mental health professionals.
4. The expectations for coaches and staff in contributing to the mental health of their athletes.
5. Referral and confidentiality policies of the sport organization.
6. Other relevant topics.

TRAINING GUIDELINES

The previous sections of this chapter provided guidelines and content about how to *educate* coaches and staff about the mental health of their athletes. This section focuses on guidelines and content concerning how to *train* these stakeholders to take specific actions regarding mental health contributions. More specifically, these guidelines and content intend to provide information you, as a practitioner, can use to equip coaches and staff with skills necessary for them to carry out their responsibilities as mental health contributors.

In this regard, the training goals to set for coaches and staff to attain—concerning their responsibilities as mental health contributors—are the following:

1. Commit to their roles and responsibilities as mental health contributors.
2. Respect the confidentiality of athletes.
3. Communicate with athletes about mental health.
4. Collaborate with mental health professionals regarding the mental health of athletes.

You can address these training goals through the active involvement of coaches and staff in planned meetings or workshops. In these settings, you can train coaches and staff on skills associated with each goal. Toward this end, you can also develop and use case studies so coaches and staff can consider how they would attain each training goal in those situations. In turn, you can provide feedback concerning their approach to each case study.

> ## Training Goal 1: Committing to Roles and Responsibilities as Mental Health Contributors
>
> This training goal centers on making sure the coaches and staff: (a) understand and follow through with their roles and responsibilities as mental health contributors; (b) adhere to those roles and responsibilities so they do not overstep them; and (c) discuss with others in the sport organization how they can contribute to the mental health of their athletes.
>
> For a coach or staff member to commit to the roles and responsibilities of a mental health contributor, they must become skilled in taking the following actions:
>
> - Recognizing that their role as a mental health contributor is not that of a licensed mental health provider. Rather, their contribution is to support the mental health of their athletes through listening and caring for them as people, over and above sport.
> - Engaging in interactions with their athletes, within the bounds of their professional competence and education.
> - Demonstrating a willingness to be a member of a larger athlete performance team dedicated to the total development of their athletes.

> ## Training Goal 2: Respecting Confidentiality of their Athletes
>
> The focus of this training goal is for each coach and staff member to maintain information related to the mental health of their athletes in confidence, unless the matter involves the health and safety of others. In this regard, it is important for coaches and staff to become skilled at taking these actions:
>
> - Recognizing that information their athletes share with them is to remain confidential and not revealed to others without the athlete's expressed permission.

- Abiding by the sport organization's policies about mental health as well as those of other related health agencies.
- Identifying the types of situations that pose a threat to the safety and well-being of each athlete and their teammates, as well as only expressing specific concerns about athletes in confidence to licensed mental health professionals.

Training Goal 3: Communicating with Athletes about Mental Health

This training goal reflects the capacity of a coach or staff member to talk with their athletes about mental health. This is especially important when one or more athletes express an interest or willingness to engage in such conversation. Such discussions may be informal or could occur as part of a one-on-one or even a group meeting.

Regarding this training goal, here are some actions for which coaches and staff can become skilled:

- Listening to the needs and concerns of their athletes when one or more of them raise the topic of mental health. Whether the athlete wishes to speak about their own mental health as an athlete or discuss a mental health topic more generally, the coach or staff member can listen non-judgmentally.
- Seeking to understand what the athlete is saying and learning to feel confident and comfortable in asking for clarification from the athlete about their expressed concern.
- Reinforcing and otherwise complimenting the athlete for bringing up the topic and letting the athlete know they, the coach or staff member, support them, in confidence.
- Searching for information about the mental health topic the athlete would like to learn more about as well as being willing to refer the athlete to a more knowledgeable source (such as a mental health professional).

Training Goal 4: Collaborating with Mental Health Professionals

This training goal involves equipping coaches and staff with skills needed to collaborate with the mental health professionals associated with the sport organization. Within this context, coaches and staff can acquire, develop, and maintain these skills:

- Attending all meetings related to the mental health of their athletes.
- Contacting an appropriate member of the mental health team to discuss concerns they have about an athlete.
- Suggesting the mental health professional look into their concerns about athletes, with a possibility of referral for assessment and intervention.
- Providing their opinions about the mental health of one or more of their athletes concerning matters of mental health.

DESCRIPTIONS OF EDUCATION AND TRAINING PROGRAMS FOR MENTAL HEALTH CONTRIBUTORS

In this section, I provide descriptions of education and training programs for coaches and staff regarding their role as mental health contributors. These are education and training programs I have designed and implemented. These descriptions offer an overview of some of the programs. You should consider these *examples* only and should not construe them as curriculum guides or program manuals.

- *Educating and training of coaches at a Division 1 university:* The purpose of this program was to provide the head coaches and assistant coaches for football and men and women's basketball teams at a Division 1 university with information about the meaning of mental health; it also focused on how they could support their student-athletes' well-being as performers and people. This program involved the coaches in three workshop sessions spaced over three weeks. During each workshop session, coaches were involved in learning about the nature and scope of mental health in sport as well as the factors likely to put their student-athletes at risk for mental health problems. They also learned how they can communicate with their athletes about mental health within and outside competitive venues.

- *Educating player development staff of a professional baseball organization:* The purpose of this program was to educate player development staff about organizational policies and procedures regarding the mental health and well-being of players. Player development staff included baseball coaches, athletic trainers, strength and conditioning coaches, and player development administrators. The program occurred over four days, one hour each day after normal field activities. During these educational sessions, participants learned about the purpose and goals of the organization's mental health framework in addition to mental health indicators that signal their awareness and concern about the mental health of players. They also learned about the nature and scope of confidentiality and how to discuss their concerns about players with the organization's mental health professionals.

- *Training the performance team of an NBA team:* The purpose of this program was to train performance team members—strength coaches, a mental skills coach, and athletic trainers—in skills that would assist them in identifying players' mental health problems. It also addressed how to approach players with their concerns, how to discuss mental health issues and concerns with players, and how to collaborate with one another in support of player mental health. This program occurred over four days, one day per week. The training time included discussion of skills, role play activities, and feedback to the performance team members.

- *Educating coaches and athletic director of a large urban high school:* The purpose of this program was to educate the athletic director and coaches of all sports regarding the following areas: (a) the definition of mental health; (b) common mental health problems of athletes; (c) how to proceed if they suspect mental health problems in their athletes; (d) communication with parents concerning mental health; and (e) how to provide support to athletes.

Practitioner Exercises

1. What has mental health of athletes meant to you? What can you do to make sure coaches, staff, and athletes learn about the meaning of mental health?
2. In what areas can you educate and train coaches and staff about mental health?
3. What are your strong points regarding educating and training coaches and others to be mental health contributors?
4. What do you need to learn or improve so you can take the lead in the education and training of coaches and others about the mental health of athletes?

Nine

This chapter provides perspectives and guidelines that can assist you in collaborating with the coaching staff of a team to create and sustain an environment conducive to the mental health of their athletes. First, it offers a rationale for creating an environment for mental health at the team level. Second, it considers the nature and scope of an environment for team mental health. Third, the chapter discusses the roles and responsibilities of coaches for establishing and sustaining a team environment conducive to mental health. Fourth, it details how to orient coaches and other staff to establishing a team environment that supports mental health. Fifth, it describes seven factors (DURABLE) for bringing positive mental health to the team level, within the context of a sport organization. The chapter concludes with practitioner exercises.

RATIONALE FOR CREATING A TEAM ENVIRONMENT CONDUCIVE TO MENTAL HEALTH

The purpose of an athletic team is for athletes, coaches, and staff to work together in order to attain common goals (Halberstam, 2005). Team goals are important to team success. Generally, team goals emphasize consistent, quality team performance. More specifically, team goals involve domains such as quality team preparation, effective communication among team members, productive interaction during competition, and collaborative responses to results.

One other area, however, that also can be a team goal—but often is not formally addressed—is the goal of fostering positive mental health. Quite often, even though there may be some discussion about mental health, the team has not considered the task of fostering mental health at the team level as a team goal.

Nevertheless, the team is a setting—an environment—in which athletes, coaches, and staff spend considerable time together, possibly

DOI: 10.4324/9781003159018-9

more time than with their families during the season (Raabe & Zakrajsek, 2017). During a season, members of the team engage in many different activities and experiences; some can be stressful and place the team at risk for mental health problems. These activities and experiences include engaging in considerable travel to and from home, pre-game preparation, participating in team meals, dealing with conflict between and among team members, experiencing lack of team cohesion, reviewing film together, and striving to work together through poor performance and/or adversity experienced by team members.

This range of activities and experiences at the team level can enhance or limit the psychological, emotional, and social well-being of athletes as team members. Thus, the team environment has potential to be one that supports mental health (Flett et al., 2017). The actions of coaches and others, coupled with the guidance of a sport psychology practitioner, can determine this kind of team environment.

NATURE AND SCOPE OF A TEAM ENVIRONMENT

We can define "team environment" as the surroundings and conditions in which team members live and operate, day-to-day, throughout the season. In essence, a team environment reflects a social setting. Thus, people—team members, the head coach and assistant coaches, and team staff—create, develop, and sustain the environment.

The environment in which the members of a team function encompasses the standards, norms, and preferences of the team. These include expectations such as (a) how team members relate to one another; (b) how they communicate within and outside practice and competitive venues; (c) how they use performance feedback to better themselves as a team; and (d) what they discuss with one another and with others outside the team.

Consideration of mental health in a purposeful manner at the team level can add value to the environment in which athletes, coaches, and staff function. More specifically, those associated with the team can leverage *team mental health*. I am using the term "team mental health" to refer to the ways team members, coaches, and staff think about their mental health and well-being (individually and collectively); it also refers to how they discuss mutual concerns about mental health and support team members experiencing mental health problems. Accordingly, the environment the team, the coaches, and others create will influence the extent to which mental health is addressed at the team level.

RESPONSIBILITIES FOR CREATING A TEAM-LEVEL POSITIVE MENTAL HEALTH ENVIRONMENT

The development and maintenance of an environment conducive to positive team mental health requires coaches and others who are part of the team to commit to fulfilling various responsibilities. These responsibilities may differ based on the person's role in the organization. In your position as a practitioner, you play a central role in bringing the matter of team mental health to the attention of coaches and staff. Relatedly, you can then proceed to guide them in taking responsibility for fostering positive team mental health, given their roles on the team.

Initially, you can encourage the team's head coach and assistant coaches to learn about what it means to create a team environment conducive to mental health. You can educate them about the rationale for team mental health (as described in the previous section of this chapter). As a practitioner, you also can urge coaches to work with you toward team mental health. You can present this task to them as a collaborative undertaking with you. This task can be facilitated based on the guidelines described in subsequent sections of this chapter.

Similarly, you can encourage athletic trainers and strength and conditioning personnel to work with you in creating a team environment supporting the mental health of their athletes. You can applaud them for the fact that they deal with the needs of the total athlete daily and on an ongoing basis. They typically constitute the front line of contacts when athletes express concerns about their mental health and overall well-being.

Additionally, you can also bring other support staff, such as clubhouse personnel and kitchen staff, into the fold to contribute to the creation of a positive environment for mental health, given their roles and responsibilities as part of the team. Finally, athletes themselves can be part of a team-level mental health initiative. For instance, a leadership team of athletes could work with you to make sure team mental health is being addressed in an appropriate manner.

ORIENTING COACHES AND OTHERS TO
A MENTALLY HEALTHY TEAM ENVIRONMENT

In order to establish and sustain a mentally healthy team environment, I have found it useful to orient coaches and others to that notion. This can be accomplished by holding an educational session with them that focuses on the following:

- *Definition of a team environment:* The standards, norms, and preferences that are part of the team, developed under the leadership of the head coach and assistant coaches.
- *Meaning of team mental health:* The psychological, emotional, and social well-being of team members that allows them to work together to deal with the competitive demands of their sport, interact productively with one another in support of consistent quality performance, and support one another as team members.
- *Nature and scope of a mentally healthy team environment:* An environment, created by coaches, staff, and athletes, that manifests positive team mental health.
- *The DURABLE steps:* An overview of seven steps to establish and sustain a team environment in support of mental health at the team levels: Discuss, Understand, Reinforce, Acquire, Build, Learn, Evaluate (Maher, 2021a).

THE DURABLE STEPS

These seven steps serve as guidelines for the practitioner as you seek to establish and sustain a team environment that supports mental health at the team level. These steps can increase the likelihood that your efforts will be successful in establishing a positive team mental health environment. By following these guidelines, you will be able to interact productively with athletes, coaches, and staff who are part of the team.

Discuss the Nature and Scope of Mental Health with Team Members

The purpose of this step is to discuss the definition of "team mental health." This discussion can occur at a meeting of team member athletes, with the coaches and staff in attendance. As a practitioner, and depending on your role in the sport organization, you can take the lead in this discussion. Alternatively, a coach can facilitate the discussion, provided this individual has been oriented to team mental health.

During discussion, the key points to address are the following:

- Mental health is an area relevant at the individual level, and it is also relevant at the team level.
- Mental health is an area that can be open to discussion among team members.
- Mental health has to do with being able to have a positive mindset, meet the daily demands of team practice and game competition, and interact productively with teammates.
- Team mental health also reflects the way the team and its members are concerned about one another as performers and people; it likewise involves their willingness to support one another not only through good times but also during adverse circumstances.

Understand the Viewpoints that Team Members Have Regarding Mental Health
After the discussion about mental health in relation to the team and its environment, the next step is to understand what the team members think about these matters. This step involves understanding their viewpoints, that is, their thoughts, opinions, and concerns about mental health.

As part of this step, take time to get a sense of the feelings of team members, coaches, and the staff associated with the team. Try to ascertain what they think about mental health—their own and that of others, including teammates. Informal contacts with the team, focus groups, and the use of a questionnaire are all means by which you can grow in understanding the team's views on mental health.

Team members will benefit from understanding the importance of mental health. Relatedly and most important, they need to sense that you and the coaches care about them with respect to individual and team mental health.

Reinforce Talk about Mental Health
The purpose of this step is to reinforce activities and behaviors coaches and others manifest related to mental health, within the context of the team. First, encourage talking about mental health among team members, coaches, and staff. As this type of discourse happens, congratulate the parties for talking about mental health.

Second, guide and encourage players and coaches not to back away from mental health discussions. This kind of guidance and encouragement is necessary since talking about mental health and listening to the viewpoints of others can be uncomfortable at times. Accordingly, those involved in these potentially uncomfortable discussions may benefit from feedback and reassurance from you as a sport psychology practitioner.

Third, it can be helpful to provide specific kinds of mental health information. This type of reinforcement can occur by providing team members and their coaches with articles and possibly guest speakers concerning mental health areas.

Fourth, you can reinforce mental health at the team level further by developing a mental health committee of team members. Charge this team member committee to propose ideas and activities that can educate team members and others about mental health and well-being.

Acquire Necessary Resources to Support Mental Health at the Team Level

The purpose of this step is to make sure that the resources necessary to support mental health at the team level are available to team members, coaches, and related team staff. These resources include the following:

- Access to licensed mental health professionals (so team members can contact them with questions and concerns).
- The development of a receptacle, such as a suggestion box, in which information about athlete mental health can be stored and then accessed by players and staff.
- Identification of offices or rooms where team members can meet in a confidential manner—individually or as a group—with mental health professionals.
- Creation of a budget that can help support mental health initiatives and activities such as necessary travel and honoraria for guest speakers.

Build Positive Expectations about Mental Health and the Team

To establish and sustain a team environment that supports mental health, those who are involved in that process need to manifest a positive outlook. Naturally, as a practitioner, this positivity can start with you. By being enthusiastic about mental health, it is likely that team members, coaches, and staff will be attentive to this kind of posture. Relatedly, they then are more likely to be receptive to team-related mental health ventures.

Regarding building positive expectations about team mental health, I have found these suggested actions valuable with professional and collegiate athletic teams:

- Make it a point to have coaches present material about mental health to their athletes. You can help guide coaches in presenting the information in their own manner, while maintaining the accuracy of the content.
- Encourage coaches and other team staff to talk about mental health in positive ways. This includes talking about mental health as reflecting the psychological, emotional, and social well-being of team members as well as that of themselves.
- Look for the small daily things that happen and that can be examples of mental health.

Learn Daily about Team Mental Health

The concept of team mental health is a new one. There certainly is no uniform definition for the notion. Therefore, it is very important to continue to learn daily about the following:

- How coaches and athletes view their mental health and the mental health of others in the sport organization as well as other locations.
- What constitutes an environment conducive to the mental health of team members, their coaches, and staff.

This kind of learning can occur through discussions with team members and others as well as through documenting that which is being learned, one day at a time.

Evaluate the Team Environment

On a regular basis, take time to determine the following about the team environment, particularly related to how it supports the mental health of team members, coaches, and staff:

- Determine what activities and initiatives are working; that is, ascertain what people are perceiving as successful in support of team mental health.

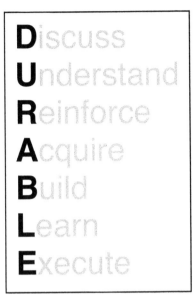

Figure 9.1 The DURABLE Steps

- Obtain reactions of team members, coaches, and staff concerning what is going well with team mental health as well as what areas will benefit from improvement.
- Make necessary adjustments.

Practitioner Exercises

1. Recall one or more of the teams for which you have provided sport psychology consultation. How was mental health addressed with these teams? What went well? What could have been done better?
2. How can you present the idea of team mental health to the team members and coaches with whom you provide sport psychology consultation?
3. What are the benefits of taking a team perspective on mental health in a sport organization?
4. How can you present the notion of team mental health to an athletic director or general manager?

Ten

This chapter provides perspectives and guidelines for the formulation of organizational-level mental health policies, plans, and procedures, in addition to guidelines for how to enact them in a sport organization. First, it offers a rationale for an organizational-level emphasis on mental health. Second, the chapter defines the nature and scope of mental health policies, plans, and procedures at the organizational level. Third, it identifies areas for the formulation and enactment of policies, plans, and procedures intended to foster the mental health of athletes and others in a sport organization. The chapter concludes with relevant practitioner exercises.

RATIONALE FOR AN ORGANIZATIONAL-LEVEL EMPHASIS ON MENTAL HEALTH

A range of individuals have leadership roles and responsibilities for the management and administration of a sport organization (Wagstaff, 2017). Depending on the type of sport organization, these individuals may include general managers, athletic directors, department heads, medical services coordinators, and other types of professionals. The roles and responsibilities of these sport organizational leaders aim at ensuring the organization provides athletes and teams with programs and services that allow for athletic accomplishments, mental and emotional development, and successful performance. To accomplish this, the provided programs and services must encompass the physical, technical, and mental domains of the development of athletes.

The design and implementation of programs and services for athletes in a sport organization necessitates that its leaders advocate for—indeed, demand—investments in the development and performance of athletes (Cruickshank & Collins, 2012). These investments comprise the acquisition and use of sufficient human, financial, and physical resources. One area that warrants a sound organizational

DOI: 10.4324/9781003159018-10

investment and crucial organizational leadership is the area of fostering the mental health of athletes, coaches, and staff (Gilmore, 2017).

More specifically, the tasks regarding mental health are manifold for leaders at the organizational level of a sport organization. These tasks include making sure the following elements are realized: (a) a systematic approach is in place for the assessment of the mental and emotional needs of athletes in relation to their mental health and well-being; (b) a process is in operation for the design and implementation of programs and services that will address the identified mental and emotional needs of athletes, coaches, and others; (c) stakeholders exhibit active involvement with regard to the formulation of policies, plans, and procedures to make certain mental health programs and services are clear and supported; (d) an evaluation action plan pertaining to the enactment of mental health policies, plans, and procedures is evident; and (e) both opportunity and a process for making revisions in programs and services based on program evaluation data exist.

These elements will not be realized in an appropriate manner, though, if they are relegated to less than priority status (Van Raalte et al., 2015). Therefore, thoughtful and purposeful policies, plans, and procedures are warranted in relation to fostering the mental health of athletes, coaches, and staff (as well as for developing a mentally healthy sport organization). These policies, plans, and procedures should increase the likelihood of positive organizational outcomes

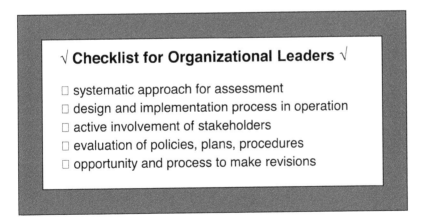

Figure 10.1 Checklist for Organizational Leaders

regarding mental health in the sport organization, thus contributing to developing a mentally healthy sport organization.

NATURE AND SCOPE OF MENTAL HEALTH POLICIES, PLANS, AND PROCEDURES

In order to formulate and enact polices, plans, and procedures supportive of the mental health of athletes, coaches, and staff in a sport organization, I have found it necessary to explain what those terms mean to sport organizational stakeholders. This explanation of terms serves as the basis to help guide organizational leaders in formulating and enacting appropriate approaches.

A *mental health policy* in support of the mental and emotional development of athletes, coaches, and staff is a course of action or principle (belief) adopted by a sport organization. The organization adopts the policy to support the mental health and well-being of athletes, coaches, and staff. More specifically, a mental health policy intends to result in one or more tangible accomplishments that will benefit the sport organization. In this regard, mental health plans and procedures enact and implement a mental health policy, once formulated.

A *mental health plan* manifests itself as a systematic approach for doing something or achieving goals related to mental health; thus, the plan should be in alignment with a particular policy. The plan is organized by goals, activities, and a way to monitor the implementation of the plan, along with a means for an evaluation of the extent to which the goals of the plan are being attained.

A *mental health procedure* is similar to a mental health plan. However, a procedure is more specific than a plan. It reflects a way of doing something that is part of a mental health policy or plan.

AREAS FOR THE FORMULATION AND ENACTMENT OF POLICIES, PLANS, AND PROCEDURES

In light of the above definitions, thoughtfully formulated and carefully enacted policies, plans, and procedures for fostering the mental health of athletes and others can benefit a range of areas in a sport organization. These areas include, but are not limited to, the following:

- Importance of mental health.
- Confidentiality.

- Leadership for mental health.
- Qualified mental health professionals.
- Mental health assessment.
- Mental health referral.
- Mental health crisis and emergency action situations.
- Coach and staff education about mental health.

The next subsections provide further descriptions as well as *examples* of mental health policies, plans, and procedures for each of those areas.

Policy about the Importance of Mental Health

An explicit policy about mental health and its importance within the context of the sport organization is valuable for two basic reasons. First, a mental health policy about the importance of mental health signifies that mental health is an integral part of the organization's operation. In other words, those who are part of the sport organization consider the notion of mental health so important that it requires a formal statement. Second, a mental health policy provides guidance to organizational leadership about what they are responsible for concerning mental health, given their roles and professional skill sets.

A mental health policy that deals with the importance of mental health in a sport organization makes the following notions explicit: (a) clarifies that mental health is an important area of the sport organization; (b) defines what the organization means by mental health; and (c) points out that the contribution to the mental health of athletes, coaches, and staff is a multidisciplinary one.

Below, I provide an example of a mental health policy statement I have used with a professional hockey organization. As we formulated this statement, we intended to make explicit that the organization was placing a premium on the importance of mental health in that organization.

Here is the formal policy statement:

- Mental health of our players, coaches, and staff is a priority for our organization. Mental health is an integral part of who we are and what we are about in relation to our players, coaches, and staff. Mental health is important because we want to make sure we address the mental and emotional needs of our players, coaches, and staff through programs and services that have been designed in conjunction with licensed mental health professionals. Within our organization, mental health is defined as the psychological, emotional, and social well-being of our athletes, coaches, and staff, where these individuals cope effectively with the demands they encounter, interact productively with others, and contribute to their respective communities. This is what is important to us, immediately and going forward.

Policy about Confidentiality

When a sport organization addresses the mental and emotional needs of athletes and others, it typically gathers, discusses, and communicates a range of information about the athletes and others. Communication of this nature involves athletes, mental health professionals, and others, including coaches and staff. For the most part, this communicated information concerns the overall development and performance of the athletes.

However, when an athlete shares information with another individual, such as a mental health professional, the athlete expects that the information shared will remain confidential between the two parties. In essence, an athlete expects the other individual will not share this information with others without the athlete's expressed written permission. Moreover, if the individual with whom the athlete shared personal information is a mental health professional, they are bound by ethical standards to keep that information in confidence.

Given both the importance of mental health and the desire to help the athlete in effective and ethical ways, it is essential to create a mental health policy related to confidentiality in the organization. Such a policy, carefully stated, will help with the provision of programs and services in ways that are effective and ethical in nature and scope.

In relation to mental health, "confidentiality" means that information an athlete and a mental health professional discuss and share is considered private between the two parties. Furthermore, the professional will not provide this information to others, in any form, without the expressed written consent of the athlete. In this sense, "confidential" means the information is restricted in its use.

There are many aspects of mental health program and service delivery in which confidentiality must be considered at the organizational level in terms of policy formulation. A policy emphasizing the importance of confidentiality is especially necessary in the following situations:

- When dealing with information that pertains to the psychological assessment of the athlete, particularly where the information is stored and who has access to it.
- When contacts between an athlete and another professional lead to documentation regarding the mental performance and overall well-being of the athlete.
- When information relates to personal discussions with sport psychologists, mental performance coaches, and mental health clinicians.

Regarding mental health of athletes within the context of a sport organization, the following is a policy statement I formulated and helped to enact in a professional baseball organization:

- When our sport psychology and mental performance team provide mental health programs and services to our players, there often will be information shared between a player and these individuals that has to do with the psychological, emotional, and social well-being of the player. The information that emanates from discussions of this type is confidential between the player and the other individual. The information is confidential because it is private and restricted to the use of the player and the other individual. The information is not to be provided to others without the expressed written consent of the player.

Policy about Leadership for Mental Health

Leadership is essential to foster the mental health of athletes in a sport organization. Sport organizational leadership regarding mental health manifests itself when leaders guide and direct the attitudes and activities of coaches and staff concerning the mental and emotional development of their athletes.

At the sport organizational level, leaders are expected to guide, direct, and communicate about mental health to athletes, coaches, and others. These leaders may be, for instance, the general manager of a professional sport franchise, the athletic director of a division of intercollegiate athletics, a director of sport medicine, or others with leadership expectations.

As a practitioner, you can shape the organizational leadership behavior of these kinds of leaders. You can do this by (a) communicating with them about the nature and scope of mental health; (b) providing them with information about mental health they can use as a basis for a policy statement; (c) educating them about the nature and scope of mental health of athletes; and (d) enhancing their knowledge about the nature and scope of mental health.

In terms of manifesting leadership for mental health in a sport organization, I share here an *example* of a leadership policy statement I have used at the collegiate level:

- The leaders of the athletic department are expected to be committed to the task of fostering the mental health of our student-athletes. This commitment is reflected in how each leader strives to increase their knowledge about mental health and how they communicate with student-athletes, coaches, and staff about the importance of mental health to them.

Policy about Qualified Mental Health Professionals

The design and implementation of mental health programs and services to athletes, coaches, and staff requires that qualified mental health professionals provide these initiatives. Accordingly, you need to formulate and enact a policy so that the sport organization employs qualified mental health professionals or uses them as contracted consultants.

"Qualified" mental health professionals who work in a sport organization meet these criteria:

- They possess graduate education and training in mental health and sport psychology.
- They possess a valid license that allows them to offer mental health services (e.g., a licensed psychologist, licensed professional counselor, or licensed clinical social worker).
- They document their accumulated professional experiences addressing the mental health needs of athletes and other adult populations.

Regarding organizational-level policy, you can place these criteria, along with other relevant criteria depending on the nature and scope of the sport organization, into a written statement. Here is an *example* of such a policy statement you could use or adapt for most professional, collegiate, and secondary school sport organizations:

- The delivery of mental health services to our athletes, coaches, and staff must occur only by means of duly licensed mental health professionals. These professionals are either employed by our organization, contracted with it, or function as recipients of referrals as part of the professional's independent practice.

In terms of mental health procedures to assure that qualified mental health providers are associated with the sport organization, consider these important steps:

- Appoint a search committee to identify qualified candidates.
- Develop and implement a strategy for assessing candidates for the available mental health positions.
- Provide guidelines for the search committee for reviewing candidate applications and interviewing candidates.
- Create a plan for the onboarding, supervision, and development of each newly hired mental health professional.

Policy about Mental Health Assessment

We can define "mental health assessment" as the process of gathering assessment information about the mental and emotional development of athletes to use as a basis for making decisions about the provision of programs and services for them. Therefore, mental health assessment is an important area for leaders of a sport organization to consider; they must also ensure that an appropriate assessment process is in operation. However, people often do not take into account mental health assessment of this nature and scope at the organizational level in terms of policy.

A policy about mental health assessment, though, clarifies and signifies the importance of such assessment. This kind of policy is best developed under the guidance of a qualified mental health professional (perhaps you) in collaboration with sport organizational leaders. A policy of this nature should provide guidance about the types of assessment the organization will use (see Chapter 6 for the various types of mental health assessments). The policy also should include information about the mental health needs assessment and mental health screening, in addition to the importance of assessment, the details of who will perform the assessments, and the people for whom the assessment is important.

Here is an example of a policy about mental health assessment I developed for use in a professional basketball setting:

- Mental health assessment is the process of gathering assessment information about the mental and emotional development needs of our athletes. Mental health professionals who are employed by and who otherwise work with us will analyze and interpret this assessment information. The assessment information then is used as a basis for the design and implementation of mental health programs for our players. Mental health assessment is an integral part of providing quality programs and services in our organization.

Policy about Mental Health Referral

We can define a "mental health referral" as a process whereby an athlete is referred to a qualified mental health professional for assessment and possible treatment of a mental health condition. The mental health professional who accepts the referral of the athlete may be an employee of the sport organization, or this practitioner may be external to the organization, such as someone in independent practice.

Before anyone can make a referral of an athlete to a licensed mental health provider, they must first discuss the need for a referral with the athlete and possibly with the parents or other relevant parties. To support and ensure that mental health referrals occur in an appropriate manner, it is useful to have an explicit policy for the sport organization.

Here is an example of this kind of policy regarding a mental health referral. I used this policy with a university athletic department:

- In our university, a student-athlete is referred for mental health services to a qualified mental health professional following discussion with the student-athlete and other relevant parties. It is our intent that due to the referral, the student-athlete can participate in additional and more specific assessment related to their mental health concern and then receive possible mental health intervention.

In some situations in a sport organization, an athlete will manifest mental health problems that require crisis or emergency action by mental health professionals and others. When these circumstances occur, it is important to have a plan in place for crisis and emergency action.

An athlete experiencing a mental health crisis demonstrates an immediate decline in performance and personal functioning. The individual may have exhibited disruptive or disturbing behavior or shown noticeable changes in appearance, behavior, or weight. They may have appeared to coaches and teammates as sad, anxious, or experiencing mood shifts. Furthermore, the athlete may be frequently angry or easily frustrated. In a crisis situation, there is a focus on communicating with the athlete and discussing with them the immediate need for mental health assistance.

An athlete who is making disturbing comments, bullying others, and engaging in aggressive behaviors detrimental to the health and safety of others is a candidate for emergency action by the mental health team. In such a situation, the mental health team likely will decide to get the athlete immediate assistance, which may include hospitalization.

To deal effectively with mental health crises and emergency situations such as those noted above, it is important for the organization to invest in an athlete mental health crisis and emergency action plan. This plan should consist of the following elements:

1. *Purpose of the plan:* To provide immediate and effective assistance to any athlete who is experiencing psychological problems that require immediate action.
2. *Core roles and responsibilities:* The individuals, such as the mental health team, who are responsible for overseeing and taking crisis and emergency actions.
3. *Process for taking actions:* Following through on the necessary steps to take actions, such as triage assessment, discussion, referral and related decisions, and follow-through.
4. *Monitoring the situation:* Keeping track of what actions have been taken and by whom, as well as tracking the outcomes of those actions.

Appendix A provides an example of a mental health emergency action plan.

The education of coaches and staff about the mental health of their athletes functions as an important aspect of the sport organization. When coaches and staff are educated about athlete mental health—that is, when they become literate about it—the likelihood increases that they will support their athletes' mental health; it also makes it more likely that they will be able and willing to provide appropriate guidance to the athletes, especially during trying times.

Hence, I recommend an organizational policy related to education because it is useful. Here is an example of one such policy:

- Our athletes will benefit from coaches and staff who are supportive of mental health. In this respect, we will provide ongoing education about mental health to coaches and staff, including education concerning how they can provide appropriate assistance to the athletes who are part of their teams.

Practitioner Exercises

1. How can you approach the administrators and leaders of the sport organizations in which you work about the value of having in place documented policies, procedures, and plans regarding mental health?
2. Which individuals in your sport organization are best suited to be part of a mental health team? Why are these individuals so suited? What kind of education and training about mental health would benefit them?
3. How would you discuss the matter of confidentiality with coaches, athletes, and others?
4. To what extent can you as a practitioner take the lead in working with sport organizational leaders and other relevant professionals in formulating a mental health crisis and emergency action plan?

Eleven

This chapter provides a framework, along with procedural guidelines, that practitioners can use when coordinating programs and services related to mental skills, life skills, and mental health in a sport organization. First, it sets forth a rationale about the importance of the coordination of these kinds of programs and services, including what is meant by program and service coordination. Second, it delineates the nature and scope of the mental skills area. Third, the chapter offers a description of the life skills domain. Fourth, it positions the area of mental health in relation to mental skills and life skills domains within the context of a sport organization and the quest for the mental and emotional development of athletes. Fifth, it addresses the supervision of mental health programs and services. Sixth, the chapter describes procedural guidelines the practitioner can use so they can implement mental skills, life skills, and mental health programs and services in a coordinated manner, with each area being complementary to and supportive of each other area. The chapter concludes with practitioner exercises.

RATIONALE FOR PROGRAM AND SERVICE COORDINATION

There are a range of programs and services a sport organization can provide that impact the mental and emotional development, mental health, and competitive performance of athletes. I have found it useful to categorize these initiatives into mental skills, life skills, and mental health domains in order to best organize these programs and services so they complement and support each other.

The nature and scope of the sport organization, though, determines exactly what programs and services will be provided in these domains. Yet regardless of what programs and services are offered, they will benefit from coordination. More specifically, the areas of mental skills, life skills, and mental health all merit coordination with one another (Fogaca, 2021). These kinds of programs and services—separately and

DOI: 10.4324/9781003159018-11

collectively, carefully designed and implemented—are likely to benefit the psychological, emotional, and social well-being of athletes who are part of a sport organization (Thelwell et al., 2006).

No uniform conception of what program and service coordination means within the context of a sport organization exists, as far as I know. Despite this, I have used the term "program and service coordination" in my professional practice in a specific and purposeful manner. I have used it as a concept to ensure my work achieves the following: (a) all programs and services in sport psychology work together so they complement one another and operate in support of the mental and emotional development of athletes; and (b) all mental and emotional program initiatives are not at odds with one another, nor do they hinder implementation efforts.

Below, I provide a definition of program and service coordination. I have found this definition helpful, as have other practitioners, in developing a mentally healthy sport organization.

- The coordination of programs and services intended to foster the mental and emotional development, mental health, and competitive performance of athletes is a process. By means of this process, professionals in a sport organization work together to make sure mental skills, life skills, and mental health programs and services meet the following criteria:
  - *Practicality:* The programs and services are designed and implemented in ways that do not disrupt organizational routines.
  - *Complementarity:* The programs and services occur in ways that enhance and connect with one another in addressing the mental and emotional needs of athletes, rather than working against or limiting how such needs are addressed.
  - *Knowledgeability:* The programs and services are implemented with the understanding of their purpose and goals by the professionals involved with them, as well as by other stakeholders.

When mental skills, life skills, and mental health programs and services are coordinated, based on the above criteria, the following individual, team, and organizational benefits are likely realized:

- The professionals involved in designing and implementing these programs and services know and accept their roles, responsibilities, and relationships, given their education, training, licenses, certifications, and skill sets.

- The staff implementing the programs and services are qualified to do so, insofar as they possess the requisite knowledge, skills, and abilities.
- Communication and collaboration occur between and among those professionals involved with the design, implementation, and evaluation of the programs and services.
- The mental health domain is considered an integral part of the mental and emotional development and performance of the athletes and is not viewed as separate from these developmental areas. In essence, mental health programs complement and support the initiatives related to the mental skills and life skills areas.

Coordination of mental skills, life skills, and mental health programs and services indeed is necessary for the development of a mentally healthy sport organization. This is because, increasingly, all the program and service offerings in these areas intend to contribute to the psychological, emotional, and social well-being of athletes, coaches, and staff.

NATURE AND SCOPE OF THE MENTAL SKILLS DOMAIN

In terms of effective program and service coordination, it is essential to define what we mean by "mental skills domain." Within the context of a sport organization, I consider the term mental skills domain as referring to capabilities that allow an athlete opportunity to develop, enhance, and maintain competitive performance. For an athlete to develop their mental skills, the individual must become knowledgeable about mental skills and then make a commitment to practice them. The motivation of the athlete to learn about and engage in mental skills, in and of itself, is likely to foster their psychological, emotional, and social well-being; thereby, even learning about mental skills contributes to the mental health of the athlete.

Mental skills are manifested by behaviors, actions, and procedures an athlete applies, typically in the performance setting. In this respect, an athlete applies specific mental skills before, during, and after competition, no matter what the performance venue. We know that a range of athletes at professional, collegiate, and secondary school levels use mental skills. Evidence exists that application of mental skills can contribute to successful competitive performance as well as mental and emotional development (Breslin et al., 2017; Fogaca, 2021). When an athlete understands and applies mental skills in a competitive performance context, they increase the likelihood that their overall well-being may very well also be enhanced (Galli & Gonzalez, 2014; Gavrilova & Donohue, 2018).

There are manifold mental skills athletes can be taught, begin to practice, and learn to apply in support of effective performance. Athletes can acquire and develop mental skills by means of programs and services at the individual, team, and organizational levels of a sport organization.

Here are examples of mental skills athletes commonly apply in professional, collegiate, and secondary school settings:

- *Goal setting:* Delineating and pursuing goals that are sport-specific and relevant to effective performance and personal development of the athlete.
- *Visualization:* Creating and using images of one's performance.
- *Self-talk:* Saying specific statements to oneself, before and during competition, that are intended to contribute to effective performance.
- *Energy activation:* Using one's emotions so one can compete at an effective level.
- *Relaxation:* Remaining calm and composed during challenging competitive settings.
- *Breathing:* Leveraging deep breathing to remain calm and in the competitive moment.
- *Focusing:* Paying attention to what matters in the competitive moment, one step at a time.
- *Relatedness to others:* Interacting purposefully and productively with coaches and teammates during competition.

In order to learn about and apply these mental skills, athletes will benefit from instructional programs. These programs may be individualized for each athlete, or the programs may occur in a group format. Only professionals who have graduate education and training in sport psychology, however, should provide mental skills programs at individual, team, and organizational levels. Such professionals may be licensed sport psychologists or mental performance coaches, depending on the nature and scope of the program.

I have been involved in the design and implementation—sometimes by myself and other times in conjunction with other practitioners—with the following examples of mental skills programs and services:

- Design and implementation of individualized athlete mental performance plans; these plans include mental and emotional goals, planned activities, and a means to monitor progress of the athlete toward the goals.
- One-on-one mental skills instruction with selected athletes in areas such as goal setting, composure, focus, and relatedness to others.
- Group educational team meetings on specific mental skills topics such as confidence, focus, composure, and resilience.
- Consultation with managers and coaches about the mental performance of athletes on their teams concerning areas such as development of effective routines, communication, and performance feedback.
- Observations of practices and games with feedback to coaches about the mental performance of their athletes.
- Staff development programs regarding the development of mental skills for their athletes as well as for themselves.
- Reviews of the progress athletes are making toward mental skills goals.

NATURE AND SCOPE OF THE LIFE SKILLS DOMAIN

It is necessary to understand the life skills domain in order to complement and support program and service coordination efforts within the context of a sport organization. More specifically, the "life skills" area refers to a set of personal development capabilities the athlete possesses that allow that individual to engage in daily life in a productive way, outside actual competition. In other words, life skills allow the athlete to be aware of personal decisions that involve their life and to engage in healthy and productive life-related choices. The athlete uses life skills outside the competitive arena and performance contexts; like mental skills, life skills can enhance the psychological, emotional, and social well-being of the athlete.

Here are examples of life skills I have covered as I've instructed athletes at the professional and collegiate levels:

- Making informed decisions about their sleep and other forms of recovery from competition.
- Avoiding people who could negatively affect an athlete's development and career.
- Making sure to remain out of physical places and locations that are not in an athlete's best interest.
- Understanding and refusing the use of substances, such as alcohol, drugs of abuse, and performance-enhancing substances.
- Relating productively with people who are positive and supportive of an athlete's personal growth and development.
- Managing stress related to living and the daily demands of life.
- Managing and making appropriate financial decisions.
- Being informed about proper diet and nutrition.

It is best to teach life skills to athletes in a step-by-step manner, either through an educational program or one-on-one counseling or a related service. There are a range of life skills that can be taught to athletes; accordingly, there are a range of professionals qualified to provide life skills programs and services (that is, many people have education and expertise in the skills areas). These professionals include, but are not limited to, licensed psychologists, nutritionists, clinical social workers, licensed professional counselors, sleep specialists, and financial services advisors.

Here are examples of life skills programs and services you or another qualified professional might provide to athletes in sport organizations:

- Group meetings and discussion with athletes and their coaches about domestic abuse and violence.
- Substance use education with a focus on the risks of using alcohol, cannabis, drugs of abuse, and performance-enhancing substances.
- Diet and nutritional counseling.
- One-on-one instruction and group meetings about coping effectively with people, places, and things that put development and performance at risk.
- Cultural transition programs, where athletes are supported in coping effectively in new cultural and ethnic environments.

- Written and verbal expression programs such as English as a second language initiatives.

NATURE AND SCOPE OF THE MENTAL HEALTH DOMAIN

The mental health domain is broad; not surprisingly, it overlaps with aspects of the mental skills and life skills domains. Hence, there is great need for coordination between and among the programs and services that comprise these domains.

The mental health of an athlete reflects the capacity of the athlete to manage themselves so they can remain in a productive state of psychological, emotional, and social well-being, thereby effectively addressing the daily demands and stressors they experience. Within the sport organizational context, practitioners can enhance the mental health of an athlete through educational programs and related services that address needs at several separate yet related levels of mental and emotional development. These levels and areas of focus for the mental and emotional development of athletes fit into a mental and emotional development framework. I have used this framework meaningfully in professional and collegiate sport organizations.

There are four levels to the framework. Within each level, the practitioner can provide specific content. Here are examples of areas of instruction at each level of the framework:

Level 1: The Athlete as a *Person*
- Clarifying the athlete's values.
- Charting a vision for personal success and meaning for the athlete.
- Understanding their unique personality.

Level 2: The Athlete as a *"Coper"*
- Dealing effectively with risk encountered as an athlete and person.
- Knowing the places and locations that are risky and not frequenting them.
- Avoiding banned and harmful substances.

Level 3: The Athlete as a *Teammate*
- Understanding and accepting one's role on the team.
- Committing to responsibilities as a teammate.
- Relating appropriately to coaches and teammates.

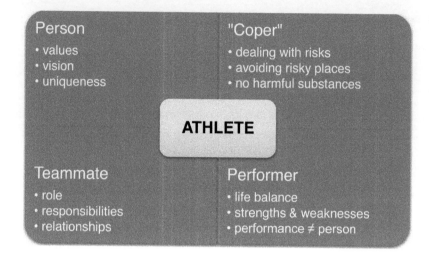

Figure 11.1 Levels of Emotional and Mental Development

Level 4: The Athlete as a *Performer*
- Balancing one's sport with one's life.
- Understanding one's strong points and areas in need of development.
- Keeping performance separate from oneself as a person.

You can design and implement mental health programs and services for the athlete at the above four levels of mental and emotional development; licensed mental health professionals, which may include you, should provide these programs and services.

Here are examples of some mental health programs and services:

- Individual mental health counseling.
- Mental health literacy programs.
- Values clarification.
- Coping skills programs.
- Team development.
- Stress management.

SUPERVISION AND RELATED MATTERS

Given the range of programs and services that can be provided in the mental skills, life skills, and mental health domains, professional supervision of the service providers plays a very important role in the sport organization, particularly concerning coordination of programs and services across the domains. Mental health coordination is a complex area; many people may need to be involved in the supervisory process and for different reasons. Thus, you must allow time to make good decisions about supervisory formats, roles, responsibilities, and relationships.

Here are two formats for professional supervision of mental skills, life skills, and mental health programs and services. They are termed "professional subject matter content supervision" and "administrative supervision."

We can define *professional subject matter content supervision* as the process of guiding and communicating with those professionals who provide mental skills, life skills, and mental health services. In this regard, the professional subject matter content supervisor needs to be an individual with a graduate degree, license, content knowledge, and skills to oversee their supervisees. This form of supervision focuses on subject matter content such as assessment, intervention methods and procedures, professional practice issues (such as confidentiality and reporting of information), and program monitoring and evaluation.

We can define *administrative supervision* as the process of overseeing whether and to what extent the mental skills, life skills, or mental health professional is functioning appropriately in relation to the policies and procedures of the sport organization. Unlike subject matter content supervision that focuses on technical content, administrative supervision deals with matters such as the professional collaborating with others, being on time for meetings, contributing to discussions, and being part of a larger performance team.

Unlike the requirements for the professional subject matter content supervisor, the individual providing administrative supervision does not need to be a licensed mental health professional. Instead, the administrative supervisor is likely to function in a leadership role such as program coordinator or departmental director. Of course, it is possible that one individual may possess the graduate education and training to serve in both capacities, that is, as both professional subject matter content supervisor and administrative supervisor.

PROGRAM AND SERVICE COORDINATION PROCEDURAL GUIDELINES

The most effective coordination of mental skills, life skills, and mental health programs and services for athletes in a sport organization occurs when it is done in a systematic manner. Accordingly, a set of program and service coordination guidelines can guide you in your work as a practitioner.

Over the years, I have developed, refined, and applied a set of procedural guidelines for the effective coordination of mental skills, life skills, and mental health programs and services. These guidelines are represented as the following tasks:

- *Clarify* the need for mental skills, life skills, and mental health programs and services for athletes.
- *Describe* the mental skills, life skills, and mental health programs and services that will be provided.
- *Identify* the providers who will implement the programs and services.
- *Delineate* supervisory roles.
- *Evaluate* program and service coordination.

Clarify the Need for Programs and Services

If you wish to coordinate mental skills, life skills, and mental health programs and services in a way that has value for athletes, then it is helpful to clarify why these offerings are needed in the first place. Your explanation also may assist in discerning how and when the programs and services should be designed and implemented.

You can clarify the need for mental skills, life skills, and mental health programs and services by considering their basic intents. These intents are:

- *Mental skills:* Equipping athletes with skills that will enable them to (a) prepare for competition so they are mentally and emotionally ready to compete; (b) engage in competition so they pay attention to what matters in the moment and execute with success; and (c) use feedback about their competitive performance so they can develop and improve.
- *Life skills:* Equipping athletes with skills so they can (a) understand life-related choices they need to make; (b) engage in effective decision-making related to their lives; and (c) monitor their daily living experiences.
- *Mental health:* Fostering the psychological, emotional, and social well-being of athletes so they can (a) cope effectively with the demands of life; (b) interact productively with others; and (c) contribute to their community.

Describe the Programs and Services

Once you have established the need for mental skills, life skills, and mental health programs and services in the sport organization, it is necessary to describe these programs and services in more detail. Consequently, athletes, coaches, staff, and other stakeholders will understand the programs and services and be able to assist, as warranted, in their coordination.

Here are steps to take when describing the programs and services:

- Identify the athletes who will be involved in mental skills, life skills, and mental health initiatives.
- For each program, state the purpose and goals of the program.
- Provide an overview of the phases and components of the program or service.
- Delineate when and where the program or service will be implemented.

Identify the Providers

The professionals responsible for the program or service actually occurring are known as the providers. To effect coordination between and among mental skills, life skills, and mental health programs and services, you must identify these providers. In addition, and most important, the providers need to be individuals qualified to offer the programs and services.

In other words, the individuals who provide mental skills programs and services must possess the education, training, and competencies to do so. Likewise, the individuals who provide life skills programs and services should possess the expertise and credentials to do so. Finally, individuals who provide mental health services need to be licensed as a psychologist, psychiatrist, clinical social worker, or other appropriately licensed professional, depending on the mental health programs and services being provided to athletes.

Delineate Supervisory Roles

As discussed earlier, it is necessary to have supervision of the individuals offering mental skills, life skills, and mental health programs and services. You need to identify the persons providing supervision in order to enhance coordination between and among programs and

Figure 11.2 Steps to Describe Programs and Services

services. You should make it clear to all involved in the organization who will be the subject matter content supervisor(s) and who will be serving as administrative supervisor(s). Relatedly, you can establish procedures so those providing supervision can meet on a regular basis to discuss the programs and services offered in the sport organization.

Evaluate Coordination

The task of evaluation of the coordination of mental skills, life skills, and mental health programs and services is an important, albeit an often-overlooked, task. However, evaluation is a professional necessity to develop and improve program and service coordination as well as other aspects of such programs and services. (Therefore, the next chapter of the book focuses on program evaluation.)

Practitioner Exercises

1. The coordination of programs and services related to mental skills, life skills, and mental health is an important, complex task. If a college director of athletics or a general manager of a professional sport franchise asked you to develop a system to make certain these areas are coordinated, how would you proceed to discuss the task with that individual?
2. Based on your experience, how do you think about the domains discussed in this chapter? How have you coordinated them in your setting? What has gone well and not so well?
3. What are challenges you can expect in the coordination of mental skills, life skills, and mental health? How and by whom can these challenges be addressed?

Twelve

This chapter provides perspectives and guidelines for the evaluation of mental health programs designed and implemented within the context of a sport organization. First, the chapter expresses a rationale for why it is important to evaluate mental health programs in sport organizations, including what is meant by mental health program evaluation. Second, it explains the nature and scope of a mental health program and offers examples describing mental health programs for athletes that would qualify as candidates for program evaluation. Third, the chapter discusses how coaches, support staff, and administrators can participate in the program evaluation process. Fourth, it gives guidelines regarding how to evaluate mental health programs intended to foster the mental health of athletes, coaches, and staff. Fifth, as part of the guidelines, the chapter details seven steps to take for the formulation and use of a mental health program evaluation plan. Finally, practitioner exercises conclude the chapter.

RATIONALE FOR EVALUATING MENTAL HEALTH PROGRAMS IN SPORT ORGANIZATIONS

Based on my professional practice experiences and that of others, I believe there are three reasons why organizational stakeholders, including sport psychology practitioners, request the evaluation of mental health programs within the context of a sport organization. The first reason is *external* in nature: someone associated with a sport organization wants an evaluation of a mental health program. The request may come from an administrator who is part of the sport organization, a member of the sport organization such as a coach or staff member, or someone who funds mental health programs and services for the sport organization. Typically, the person makes an external request for the mental health program evaluation so the stakeholders can learn

DOI: 10.4324/9781003159018-12

about the program's effectiveness and obtain a sense of the program's value for the sport organization and its athletes.

A second reason people request a mental health program evaluation is essentially *political*: someone—often an athletic administrator or board member—wants an evaluation of a sports-related mental health program because they believe it will benefit them in the eyes of others. For instance, the individual might make this kind of request when they have read about athletes and their mental health; for personal reasons, the individual wants to be associated with this kind of initiative. In particular, the individual may desire to "look good" to others, perhaps the media, through requesting the evaluation of a mental health program.

The third reason for conducting a mental health program evaluation is the most important in my judgment: *expected professional practice*. I recommend this reason as the motivation to evaluate a mental health program in a sport organization, even if there are no requests to do so from stakeholders. My recommendation stems from the belief that any mental health program in a sport organization should be evaluated as part of one's professional practice in sport and performance psychology. If we design and implement a mental health program, then we practitioners should engage in program evaluation as our professional responsibility. Toward that end, we evaluate the mental health program to obtain information so we can learn about the benefits the program seems to possess for its participants and utilize the resulting evaluation information as a means for making decisions about the continuous development and improvement of the program.

The continuous development and improvement of a mental health program is particularly important. This task is based on several presuppositions:

- The mental health of athletes, coaches, and staff is an important aspect of the sport organization. Basically, these individuals are people over and above their roles as performers. Therefore, programs and services to support their mental health are essential. These initiatives need to be developed and improved so that they can be the best possible ones for the sport organization.
- If a mental health program is to be developed and improved in any organization, including a sport organization, then a plan for evaluation is a necessity. Without a mental health program evaluation

plan, it is impossible to obtain trustworthy and contextual information about the program.

- The results of a mental health program evaluation can lead to identification of the strong points of the program; the results also can pinpoint areas for program improvement. This evaluation information thus can lead to action for further enhancement of the mental health of athletes and others.

RECOGNIZING THE NATURE AND SCOPE OF A MENTAL HEALTH PROGRAM

It is important to explain to stakeholders exactly what a "mental health program" is in order to conduct an evaluation of a mental health program that is part of a sport organization. Otherwise, you and the stakeholders—those who will be affected by data collection and/or involved in evaluation activities—may not know how to think about and focus the evaluation.

Throughout this book, we have been taking a systems approach to fostering the mental health of athletes, coaches, and staff as a means for developing a mentally healthy sport organization. From a systems vantage point, mental health programs occur at individual, team, and organizational levels of the sport entity. In many if not most instances, mental health programs span a range of psychological domains. Therefore, there is no definitive list of mental health programs; rather, these programs will vary depending on purpose and goals and the sport organization.

For the purpose of planning and conducting a program evaluation, though, we can define a *mental health program* in a sport organization as follows:

- An organized configuration of resources utilized at individual, team, and organizational levels and intended to foster the mental and emotional development and well-being of athletes and others in relation to performance and life.

The resources that comprise a mental health program are many. A program evaluation focuses on the utilization of these resources. These resources include: (a) *human resources*, such as athletes, coaches, and staff, who participate in or are affected by the program; (b) *technological resources* such as methods, plans, procedures, and

Table 12.1 Utilization of Resources in a Mental Health Program (According to Evaluation Information)

	Strong	Weak	N/A	Comments
Human resources				
Technological resources				
Informational resources				
Physical resources				
Fiscal resources				
Temporal resources				
Other				

services that are core aspects of the program; (c) *informational resources* such as policies, eligibility criteria, and program goals; (d) *physical resources* such as meeting rooms and equipment; (e) *fiscal resources* such as program budgets and sources of funding; and (f) *temporal resources*, which represent the amount of time allotted to the program. For a mental health program to have value to a sport organization as well as to those who benefit from the program (e.g., athletes and coaches), these program resources must be utilized in purposeful and effective ways.

There is no one-size-fits-all mental health program for athletes. However, no matter how large or small the program may be in terms of its nature and scope, I highly recommend you make clear the exact nature and scope of the program that will be evaluated. You can achieve such clarity about what constitutes that particular mental health program by identifying and describing its program design elements (Maher, 2012, 2021a). The design elements of a sport-related mental health program are as follows:

1. Title of the program.
2. The sport organization in which the program is embedded.
3. Program personnel: administrators, staff, consultants.
4. The athletes for whom the program is designed.
5. The athletes' mental and emotional needs the program is addressing.
6. The purpose and goals of the program: the mental and emotional areas in which the athletes will acquire, develop, and apply skills.
7. The components of the program: the specific activities, methods, procedures, and services that will be implemented with the athletes.

I have been involved in the following *examples* of types of mental health programs for athletes, coaches, and staff that have undergone program evaluation:

- Personal development program for athletes.
- Mental health individual counseling program for athletes.
- Mental health literacy program for coaches and staff.
- Mental performance enhancement program for athletes involved in long-term physical rehabilitation.
- Substance use educational program for athletes.
- Resilience training program for athletes and coaches.
- Professional self-management program for coaches and support staffs.
- Mental health leadership program for athletic directors.

PARTICIPATION IN THE EVALUATION OF MENTAL HEALTH PROGRAMS

If you want your evaluation of a mental health program in a sport organization to result in information that can lead to program development and improvement, then I propose you frame the task as a program evaluation rather than a research project. By so doing, people view the program evaluation in a broad-based manner, as the process of obtaining and analyzing information about the value of the program for its participants and for the sport organization. You can then use the resultant information as a basis for the continuous development of the mental health program (the next section of the chapter explains how to do this).

To obtain information about the value of a mental health program within a sport organization, it is important to have a range of individuals involved in the data collection and information gathering process. This variety of contributors prevents the focus of information generated about the program from being too limited in nature and scope for continuous development and improvement purposes.

As part of the program evaluation, you should ask many individuals—coaches, administrators, athletes, and other stakeholders—to provide their opinions and render comments about the program. Request that they share their opinions about the strong points of the mental health program as well as where and how they think the program can be improved. These stakeholders can participate through interviews, focus groups, questionnaires, informal discussions, and other forms of interpersonal contact.

Broad participation of this nature and scope in the evaluation of mental health programs is in line with the philosophy that the fostering of mental health in a sport organization is the responsibility of a range of stakeholders. Through their involvement in being interviewed, completing questionnaires, and participating in other kinds of evaluation activities, these stakeholders are contributing to the development and improvement of mental health initiatives in their sport organization.

CONDUCTING A MENTAL HEALTH PROGRAM EVALUATION

If you want to conduct a mental health program evaluation in a sport organization in a way that results in helpful information for the program's continuous development and improvement, then I recommend you follow several separate yet interrelated steps:

1. Define "mental health program evaluation."
2. Establish a mental health program evaluation team.
3. Decide which mental health program will be evaluated.
4. Formulate a mental health program evaluation plan.
5. Implement the mental health program evaluation plan.
6. Construct a mental health program evaluation report.
7. Communicate and use the mental health program evaluation information.

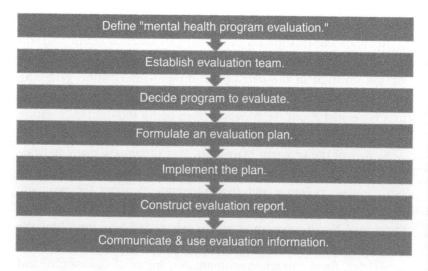

Figure 12.1 Steps to Conduct a Mental Health Program Evaluation

Each of these steps will be discussed in the remaining sections of this chapter.

STEP 1: DEFINE WHAT "MENTAL HEALTH PROGRAM EVALUATION" MEANS

Before you can conduct a mental health program evaluation in a sport organization, it is essential to define "mental health program evaluation." Defining the term will make clear to those involved in the evaluation process, as well as other organizational stakeholders, what mental health program evaluation means and entails. In turn, this understanding sets the stage for these individuals and groups to become familiar with—and to participate actively in—the process that constitutes mental health program evaluation.

Here is a definition of mental health program evaluation that I have used in my professional practice in a range of sport organizations:

- Mental health program evaluation in a sport organization is a process that involves gathering and considering information about a clearly described mental health program. The resulting evaluation information then can be used to make decisions about the program's strong points and to identify how the program can benefit from continuous development and improvement. Accordingly, the process of conducting the program evaluation as well as using the resultant evaluation information contributes to the overall task of fostering the mental health of athletes, coaches, and staff.

When we unpack this definition of mental health program evaluation, important points become apparent. First, program evaluation is a process, that is, purposeful evaluation activities that occur in step-by-step manner, over the time frame of the evaluation. The use of the process stands in contrast to an evaluation construed solely as the administration of a survey, a point in time measurement, or a research project.

Second, the definition focuses on gathering and using information about a clearly described mental health program. Thus, to conduct a meaningful program evaluation, the actual program description must allow evaluative information to be obtained about the program. Otherwise, what is being evaluated will not be clear to all concerned.

Third, the definition highlights a focus on using the resulting evaluation information to make decisions about how to develop and improve the program. This kind of focus stands in contrast to a research focus (where an intervention is assessed in relation to a research hypothesis).

Fourth, when a mental health program evaluation occurs in a practical and meaningful way, the process and resulting evaluation information contributes to the fostering of mental health in the sport organization.

Given your local circumstances, you may want to revise this definition for your context. However, no matter what the situation, make sure that it is clear to all concerned what you mean by "mental health program evaluation" within the context of the sport organization in which you are engaged as part of your professional practice.

STEP 2: ESTABLISH A MENTAL HEALTH PROGRAM EVALUATION TEAM

There are two basic ways to conduct a mental health program evaluation within the context of a sport organization. One way is for an individual knowledgeable about and experienced in program evaluation to oversee and conduct the evaluation. This individual may be you as a sport psychology practitioner, or it could be someone in a consulting role whose practice lies outside the organization.

Another way to conduct a mental health program evaluation is to establish a mental health program evaluation team. I recommend taking a team approach to mental health program evaluation, if possible. Through a team approach, the evaluation process benefits from a range of perspectives.

The purpose of a mental health program evaluation team is to involve a variety of organizational stakeholders in the formulation of a program evaluation plan; it also includes them in the oversight of the implementation of the plan (see the ensuing sections of this chapter). The members of the mental health program evaluation team could include one or two mental health professionals, a coach, support staff member, and an administrator. The head of the team should be a professional (perhaps you) with knowledge and experience in conducting mental health program evaluations.

Once you have established the purpose of the evaluation team and identified the team members, they can work in collaboration on the formulation and implementation of a mental health program evaluation plan. Toward that end, steps three to seven of our mental health program evaluation steps provide guidelines concerning how the program evaluation team can proceed collaboratively.

STEP 3: DECIDE WHICH MENTAL HEALTH PROGRAM WILL BE EVALUATED

This step clearly is necessary to conduct a mental health program evaluation in a sport organization: decide which program to evaluate and why. This requires being able to identify the actual program and its components (programs and services) that will be part of the evaluation.

In any sport organization, several mental health programs, services, and initiatives may be candidates for evaluation. Making decisions about which ones to evaluate is not an easy or straightforward task, especially when there are numerous possibilities. Here are some guidelines based on my professional practice in conducting mental health program evaluations in sport organizations:

1. Identify the program, service, or other initiative that has been a primary focus during the past year. That is, this is the program in which the most sessions occurred or where most athletes have been program participants.
2. Decide whether this particular program is ready for evaluation. If the program's purpose and goals and process, or its components, are unclear, then any attempt at evaluation of the program is unlikely to result in helpful information that could be used for program development and improvement.
3. If there is more than one program or service that seems ready to be evaluated, consider the extent to which more than one program should be evaluated. It is necessary to ponder this since the time and individuals needed to evaluate more than one program may not be available.

Here are a few examples of some titles of mental health programs and services that may be candidates for program evaluation:

- Player personal development program.
- Mental performance program enhancement for athletes.
- Mental skills program for athletes involved in physical rehabilitation.
- Mental health assessment services.
- Mental health literacy program for coaches and staff.

It is important to formulate and document a plan to conduct a mental health program evaluation that can be used for program development and improvement. A mental health program evaluation plan, carefully formulated, will spell out the program to be evaluated as well as why, when, how, and by whom.

I have found the following activities useful in formulating a mental health program evaluation plan:

- Specify the purpose of the mental health program evaluation.
- Describe the design of the mental health program that will be evaluated.
- Delineate program evaluation questions on which data will be collected.
- Select data collection methods and procedures to answer the questions.
- Identify the program evaluation staff.

Let's look at each of these activities for a mental health program evaluation plan in more detail.

Specify the Purpose of the Mental Health Program Evaluation

If you are going to conduct a mental health program evaluation in a sport organization, your time is well spent letting stakeholders know about the purpose of the evaluation. Specifying the purpose is important because the term "program evaluation" can mean different things to different people and thus easily can be misinterpreted.

I have found the following definition of "mental health program evaluation" to be informative for coaches, staff, administrators, and athletes in a variety of sport organizations. Further, this statement of purpose should be part of the mental health program evaluation plan:

- Mental health program evaluation is the process we will be using during the year. The process will involve gathering information about the mental health program in the form of questionnaires, focus groups, and other methods. This information will be gathered from coaches, staff, administrators, and athletes during the year. We will use the information to learn about areas of the program that are working well and areas in need of improvement.

Naturally, you can adjust this statement of purpose regarding dates and the context of the sport organization.

Describe the Design of the Mental Health Program that Will Be Evaluated

To evaluate a mental health program in a sport organization, it is necessary to put the program into written form so that all concerned will know the focus of the evaluation. This means you must describe the program so it can be placed into "evaluable form." An evaluable program design consists of the following elements:

- Title and relevant context of the mental health program.
- Overview of the program's participants.
- Purpose and goals of the program.
- Program organization.
- Program personnel.

Appendix B contains a description of a mental health program I have implemented with a range of professional sports teams. This *example*, which includes each of the design elements, should give you a sense of what is included for each element as a program design description. (A more detailed version of the design of this specific program is available from me, upon request.)

Delineate the Program Evaluation Questions on which Data Will Be Collected

A program evaluation question is a practical way to focus an evaluation of a mental health program (once the program design has been described). An answer to a program evaluation question can provide information that will allow you to make an evaluative judgment about a mental health program as that program is designed and implemented in a sport organization.

When the purpose of the evaluation of a mental health program in a sport organization is gathering information for the continued development and improvement of the program, it is important to delineate program evaluation questions. These questions must be ones evaluators can answer through their evaluation.

Here are program evaluation questions I have found to be useful when gathering evaluation information for development and improvement of a mental health program:

1. *Who participated in the mental health program?* This question is important when you want to gather information about the extent to which those who participated in the program did so and to what extent they attended.
2. *How was the mental health program implemented in relation to how the program was designed?* This question is important when you want to find out exactly what happened in the program, including whether and to what extent the program deviated from its program design.
3. *What were the reactions of individuals to the program?* This question is important to answer when you want to know what individuals thought about the program. These individuals might include people such as the athletes who participated in the program, program personnel, coaches, and administrators.
4. *What benefits have accrued to those who participated in the program?* This question has to do with program benefits. A "program benefit" is something considered valuable to the program participant. Depending on the program and its program design description, these benefits may include (a) specific goals participants have attained in relation to the program; (b) what participants have learned during the program; and (c) how participants have applied what they learned during the program to their sport or life.

Select Data Collection Methods and Procedures to Answer the Questions

Once you have delineated the program evaluation questions, the next task is to choose how to gather data to answer each question. This means selecting or developing data collection methods and procedures. Here are several methods and procedures I have found to be helpful in gathering data to answer program evaluation questions as part of the mental health program evaluation in a sport organization:

- Reviewing program records documents.
- Administering a survey instrument or questionnaire.
- Conducting a focus group.
- Engaging individuals in interviews.
- Observing the program in action.

Each of these methods and procedures can answer specific questions about the program. To illustrate how these methods can be used regarding specific program evaluation questions, I offer several examples below of questions and methods that I have found to be productive in gathering useful information. Though I previously presented these questions with a rationale for their importance, here I explain how you can find answers to these questions.

1. *Who participated in the mental health program?* A review of attendance records can answer this question, and such a review is all that may be needed. However, if the records reveal that attendance was not 100% and some participants dropped out of the program, you could ask the participants via a confidential survey or through discussion to explain their reasons for their lack of full program participation.
2. *How was the mental health program implemented?* Three methods and procedures can answer this question. The first method is a review of the mental health program design. This written description of the program can serve as an anchor point for evaluating the extent to which the program occurred relative to its design. A second approach involves observing the program as it is being implemented to assess if the phases of the program are being implemented (and as planned). A third method is to conduct individual interviews with program personnel to learn what aspects of the program could and could not be implemented.
3. *What were the reactions of individuals to the mental health program?* This question can be answered in several ways. First, individual athletes and teams who have participated in the program can be involved in a focus group to discuss their opinions about the program. A second method is to ask the program participants to complete a survey or reaction form about the program, particularly its strong points and limitations, as well as to share their thoughts on how the program can be improved. In addition, you can use a focus group and a survey method with those individuals who designed and implemented the program.
4. *What benefits have accrued to those who have participated in the mental health program?* This question can be answered when there is an interest in the following kinds of data collection variables: (a) the extent

to which program participants have attained the educational or skill-oriented goals of the program; (b) what knowledge and skills program participants, such as athletes, have applied to their athletic or life performance; and (c) the opinions of program participants in terms of how they believe they have benefited from the program. If a program goal was stated in a clear and measurable manner in the program plan, it is possible via a goal attainment rating scale to have program participants and others rate the degree of goal attainment. In gathering data about what program participants have learned during the program, you can ask participants to list their viewpoints toward learning as part of a questionnaire. Likewise, as part of a questionnaire or through interviews, you can ask program participants to make specific comments concerning how the program benefitted them.

Identify the Program Evaluation Staff

You can identify the professionals who are going to participate in and conduct the mental health program evaluation as "program evaluation staff." Thus, a program evaluation staff may consist of the following persons:

- *Director:* A mental health professional who is knowledgeable about the mental health program and has expertise to oversee and direct evaluation activities.
- *Data collectors:* Individuals responsible for gathering data to answer program evaluation questions.
- *Data analysts and report writers:* Individuals involved in analyzing the resultant data and working with the director to prepare the mental health program evaluation report.

STEP 5: IMPLEMENT THE MENTAL HEALTH PROGRAM EVALUATION PLAN

Once the program evaluation team (or relevant others) has formulated and agreed to a mental health program evaluation, implementation of the plan becomes the priority task. In this regard, the following activities can facilitate the implementation of the evaluation plan:

- Discuss the nature and scope of the plan with those who will participate in it.

- Understand their viewpoints about the plan, such as its timing and use of the resulting information.
- Reinforce their participation in evaluation activities.
- Acquire the necessary resources so the plan will be implemented as intended.
- Build enthusiasm for the plan and its purpose.

STEP 6: CONSTRUCT A MENTAL HEALTH PROGRAM EVALUATION REPORT

A mental health program evaluation report does not have to be a lengthy document or treatise about the evaluated program. Rather, the report should provide evaluation information that informs the report's reader about the program, including its strong points as well as places where it could be developed and improved.

Toward that end, here is a format for a mental health program evaluation report that I have found useful in communicating information about a mental health program:

1. Purpose of the report: Provide information for making decisions about the development and improvement of the program.
2. Report is submitted to _____ by _____ on _____.
3. Description of the program design evaluated.
   a. Title of the program.
   b. Overview of program participants.
   c. Purpose and goals of the program.
   d. Organization of the program: Phases/components, content and methods, sequence and timing of program activities.
4. Answers to the program evaluation questions.
   a. Who participated in the program?—include participants' level of competitive experience, education, ethnicity, etc.
   b. How was the program implemented?—frequency, intensity, duration relative to the design of the program.
   c. To what extent were the goals of the program attained?
   d. How did program participants and others react to the program?
   e. What are the strong points and limitations of the program?
   f. How can the program be further developed and improved?
5. Program evaluation protocol: The methods, instruments, and procedures used to answer the evaluation questions.
6. Recommendations for program development and improvement.

STEP 7: COMMUNICATE AND USE THE MENTAL HEALTH PROGRAM EVALUATION INFORMATION

A program evaluation plan might be considered a waste of time and effort unless the evaluators communicate evaluation information and use that information to support the continuous development and improvement of the mental health program. To communicate and use the resulting program evaluation information effectively, the mental health evaluation team must address the following questions:

- Who in the sport organization will receive the mental health program evaluation information?
- How will this information be communicated?
- When will communication occur?
- How will organizational stakeholders be involved in using this information for program planning purposes?

(Chapter 13 will offer answers to these questions and related matters.)

Practitioner Exercises

1. What experiences have you had in conducting or otherwise participating in a program evaluation in sport psychology or human services domains? How did you engage in these experiences? What went well and not so well, and what did you learn?
2. If the sport organization in which you are either employed or with whom you consult asked you, as a sport psychology practitioner, to design and implement an evaluation of a mental health program in the sport organization, how and why would you proceed?
3. What does mental health program evaluation in sport mean to you? If a sport psychology association asked you to discuss this topic, can you describe the nature and scope of that type of presentation?

Making Decisions about the Continuous Development and
Improvement of Mental Health Programs in
Sport Organizations

Thirteen

This chapter provides perspectives and guidelines for making decisions about the continuous development and improvement of mental health programs for athletes and others in a sport organization, based on program evaluation information. First, it offers a rationale for why it is necessary to make mental health program decisions in a purposeful, informed, and systematic manner. Second, the chapter discusses what it means to develop and improve mental health programs in a sport organization (i.e., parameters). Third, it gives guidelines and a framework for communicating and using mental health program evaluation information as a basis for making informed program decisions. Practitioner exercises conclude the chapter.

RATIONALE FOR MAKING DECISIONS ABOUT THE CONTINUOUS DEVELOPMENT AND IMPROVEMENT OF MENTAL HEALTH PROGRAMS

The task of fostering mental health in a sport organization is not a static one; rather, it is a fluid and dynamic task. As information and data about the mental and emotional needs of athletes as well as the results of mental health program evaluations become available, you can make informed decisions regarding mental health programs in those settings. Consequently, making such decisions about mental health programs using program evaluation and related information can lead to changes and adjustments to the programs, thereby contributing to the development of a mentally healthy sport organization.

Without a doubt, the changes or adjustments that need to be made in a mental health program require informed decisions, and such decisions require program evaluation information. These mental health program decisions may include the following: (a) keeping the program the same, without any changes in its design or operation; (b) making adjustments in elements of the program, such

DOI: 10.4324/9781003159018-13

as changes in program methods and procedures; (c) reducing or expanding the program in size and scope (in terms of number of participants or components); (d) terminating the program; and/or (e) other relevant programmatic decisions.

Mental health programs are not static entities; they are not laboratory research projects, where things can be held constant and controlled via such means as randomization. Rather, mental health programs are an organized configuration of resources intended to enhance the psychological, social, and emotional well-being of athletes and others; they occur in specific contexts with specific athletes (Rice et al., 2019). Therefore, it is not surprising, but rather expected, that mental health programs will require changes and revisions once they have been implemented. Consequently, the continuous development and improvement of mental health programs is an important area within a sport organization (Reardon et al., 2019). Ongoing decisions need to be made about mental health programs, and practitioners and other stakeholders should be involved in making these decisions and taking action using program evaluation information (Maher, 2021a).

I use the terms "continuous development" and "improvement of a mental health program" here for two basic reasons. First, it is best to recognize that any human service program—including mental health programs for athletes—can continue to get better. It may be helpful to think of the improvement of the mental health program as similar to the development and improvement of an individual or a team: both require continuous development. Second, for a mental health program to get better (that is, to develop and improve), decision-makers need evaluation information about the program. This information must be available to decision-makers on a continuous basis and in a systematic manner, not in a random way.

PARAMETERS OF CONTINUOUS DEVELOPMENT AND IMPROVEMENT OF A MENTAL HEALTH PROGRAM

In terms of a mental health program, I want to define what I mean by "continuous program development and improvement," and "decisions." These distinctions help clarify how these terms are used in relation to making decisions about a mental health program.

"Continuous" refers to being ready to make changes, at any time, in the evolution of a mental health program. For instance, sometimes a change in the program needs to happen before participants have completed the program; otherwise, participants will not receive the full value of the program.

"Program development" reflects a process of being able to add new features to the program, based on credible program evaluation information and other relevant information. Similar but different, "program improvement" uses program evaluation information to give the program something new, something that will add value to the program and its participants. This new something was not part of the program's initial design.

"Decisions" have to do with choices you must make between alternative ways to proceed with the continuous development and improvement of a mental health program.

Continuous program development and improvement of mental health programs relates, quite readily, to the design of the programs. Some examples of how you might continue to develop and improve a mental health program are the following: (a) expanding the number of athletes who can participate in the program; (b) adding new policies, criteria, and goals that will make the program more effective and efficient; (c) revising methods and procedures for instructing and involving athletes in the program; (d) adding additional staff to the program; and (e) eliminating a component of the program determined to lack value.

FRAMEWORK FOR THE CONTINUOUS DEVELOPMENT AND IMPROVEMENT OF A MENTAL HEALTH PROGRAM

A systems approach framework enhances the task of making good decisions about the continuous development and improvement of a mental health program in a sport organization. I have used this systems approach when working with sport organizational stakeholders to decide how to develop and improve a mental health program.

Here are the steps of the framework for using evaluation information as a basis for the continuous program development and improvement of a mental health program:

1. Identify the mental health program and its decision-makers.
2. Understand the design of the mental health program.

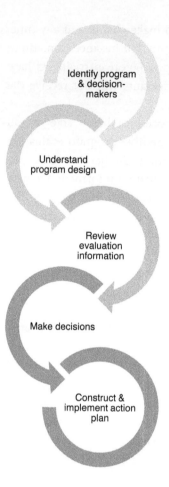

Figure 13.1 Framework for Using Evaluation Information for Continuous Program Development and Improvement of a Mental Health Program

3. Review program evaluation and related information about the program.
4. Make decisions about the program.
5. Construct and implement an action plan.

We now will look at each one of these steps in more detail.

Identify the Mental Health Program and Its Decision-Makers

This first step identifies the mental health program that has already undergone a program evaluation, along with the individuals who will be making decisions about the continuous development and improvement of the program. It is important to identify the mental health program about which you'll be making decisions because you cannot assume that all stakeholders involved in making decisions and taking actions concerning the mental health program actually will be familiar with the program.

When identifying the mental health program for which you'll be making decisions about its continued development and improvement, I have found it useful to make sure people understand the title of the program and its content, as well as the program's target population. Here are some examples from my files:

- Personal development program for professional basketball players.
- Mental health program for student-athletes in a university.
- Mental health education program for coaches and staff of a professional soccer franchise.

At this time, it is also necessary to identify the individuals likely involved in making decisions about the mental health program. Depending on the program, these individuals may be the following:

- You, as a sport psychology practitioner.
- Program staff.
- Mental health team.
- Athletic director or administrator.
- Funder of the program.

Understand the Design of the Mental Health Program

In order to make decisions and take actions for developing and improving a mental health program, decision-makers must understand the design of the program. Thus, this step provides a way of looking at the program so discussion can occur, leading to informed decisions about how to develop and improve the program.

I have found the most effective and efficient way to accomplish this task is to delineate the program's design elements. These are the essential aspects of the program. (If, during the design process, you formulated a program evaluation plan to evaluate the program, then you can refer to that plan, since it already has described the program.)

Within the context of delineating the program's design, here are important elements of a mental health program:

- The athletes or other target population for whom the program was designed and who were its participants.
- The purpose and goals of the program.
- The organization of the program in terms of the sequence, timing, and content of program activities along with its methods and procedures.
- The location, facilities, and timing of the program.
- The personnel involved in the program.

Review Program Evaluation and Related Information

Once decision-makers understand the design of the program, the next step is to review the program evaluation information generated about the program as well as other relevant information.

Program evaluation information typically is included in a program evaluation report. As I detailed in Chapter 12, a program evaluation report should include the following kinds of information:

- A description of the evaluated program.
- Who participated in the program—that is, the target population.
- How the program was implemented in terms of methods, procedures, content, activities, and personnel.
- How program participants reacted to the program.
- The extent to which program goals were attained.
- The strong points of the program as well as areas that require development and improvement.

In addition to the information contained in a program evaluation report, other information pertaining to the program may be available. This information also may be important to review as a basis for decision-making. This information may include prior evaluation reports, unsolicited viewpoints about the program received outside a program evaluation, and other such relevant information.

I have found that once you have considered the program evaluation and related information—but before making decisions about the program—it is useful to think about and answer these questions:

- What did I learn about the mental health program that I did not know prior to reviewing the evaluation and related information?
- What seem to be the strong points of the program?
- What areas of the program could benefit from change?

After pondering these questions, those involved now are ready to contribute to making decisions about the program.

Make Decisions about the Program

A decision-making structure must be established whenever it is necessary to make decisions about how to develop and improve a mental health program. This structure will make clear who is going to be involved, in what manner, and based on what information, in contributing to decisions about program development and improvement.

Here is an example of a program decision-making structure that I have found to work very well:

- Names and roles of the stakeholders involved in program decision-making: e.g., program coordinator, administrator, coaches, and/or athletes as program participants (who).
- The information the stakeholders will use as a basis for providing opinions about the program: evaluation report, testimonials, opinions, and other information (what).
- The way decisions about the program will be made: consensus or vote (how).
- When program decisions are to be made: specific date or time frame (when).

Once the stakeholders have reviewed the information about the program, they are ready to discuss their viewpoints then make decisions about the continuous development and improvement of the mental health program. Within that context, here are *examples* of possible decisions they may make about their program:

1. Making changes to the number and type of athletes who can participate in the program.
2. Clarifying the eligibility criteria for being allowed to participate in the program.
3. Describing the purpose and outcome goals in more specific and measurable ways.
4. Altering the sequence and timing of program phases or activities.
5. Providing supervision to staff implementing the program.
6. Making revisions and changes in methods and procedures used with program participants.
7. Identifying alternative locations where the program may be held.
8. Developing a practical way of monitoring the progress of program participants in relation to program goals.

In addition to the above, three other decisions that can be made about a mental health program are: (a) expand the program to other locations; (b) curtail the use of the program at some sites; and/or (c) plan for the termination of the program.

Construct and Implement an Action Plan

Once the decision-makers have determined how to develop and improve a mental health program, a final essential step is necessary. This step involves constructing a program action plan and then committing to implement it.

A program action plan serves as a means to specify what actions need to be taken in order to ensure the decisions to develop and improve the program will be made. A program action plan, in essence, is a document that spells out the following:

- Description of the program actions to be taken.
- Individuals responsible for taking these actions.
- Time frame when the actions need to be carried out.
- Deliverables that will document that the actions have occurred.

Table 13.1 is an example of an action plan for the development and improvement of one of my mental health programs.

Table 13.1 Action Plan for Personal Development Program for Basketball Players on a Professional Team

Program development and improvement actions	Implement the program during the beginning of training camp
	Refine the session of the program on values clarification and include updated clarification worksheets
	Revise participant session follow-up form to include both additional suggestions for activities between sessions and program staff contact information
	Add items to the personal development checklist concerning self-confidence and growth mindset
Individuals responsible for program development and improvement actions	Team sport psychologist
	Director of the performance team
Time frame	June–August (before training camp begins)
Deliverables	Confirmation of time frame for the program at the start of training camp
	New values clarification worksheets
	Updated personal development checklist
	Additional activities between sessions

Practitioner Exercises

1. What experiences have you had with the development and improvement of mental health programs in sport organizations? How do you regard these experiences? To what extent have you learned about the program? What did you learn about yourself?
2. What types of organizational stakeholders are likely to facilitate or to inhibit making decisions about the continuous development and improvement of mental health programs? Why?
3. What might you suggest or do in order to get decision-makers to review a program evaluation report, especially if they seem reluctant to engage in it?

Conclusion

Fourteen

COMMENTS AND NEXT STEPS

This chapter reflects on the information covered in the preceding chapters of the book. First, it offers concluding comments about the task of fostering the mental health of athletes, coaches, and staff in sport organizations by means of a systems approach. Second, it summarizes the process of developing a mentally health sport organization at individual, team, and organizational levels. Third, the chapter delineates a systems approach checklist for developing a mentally healthy sport organization that practitioners can use; the checklist also functions as a way of summarizing foundational aspects of the book. Fourth, the chapter provides thoughts regarding how practitioners can remain curious about the parameters of mental health as well as how they can take charge of their professional development concerning fostering mental health in sport organizations.

SETTING THE TONE FOR FOSTERING MENTAL HEALTH
IN SPORT ORGANIZATIONS

The task of fostering mental health in a sport organization is not an easy one. From my experiences with this task, the question of how to address mental health is itself a complex issue—challenging, but doable. The nature and scope of the task of fostering mental health in a sport organization, therefore, will vary across sport organizations and contexts. Without doubt, practitioners need to consider and deal with many people, places, and things regarding athlete, coach, and staff mental health. The task is indeed a valuable one that also can be engaging and meaningful for practitioners.

Throughout this book, I have presented and covered a range of material related to mental health at individual, team, and organizational levels, using a systems approach. I hope you have benefitted

DOI: 10.4324/9781003159018-14

from the book in some way—perhaps in many ways—as you proceed to address the mental and emotional needs of athletes, coaches, and staff in the sport organization in which you are employed or work as a contracted consultant.

Here, I would like to mention again some beliefs that we as practitioners must keep in mind. In my professional judgment, these beliefs are key to successfully developing a mentally healthy sport organization:

- Fostering mental health of athletes, coaches, and staff in a sport organization is a multi-level task in nature and scope. The task requires attention, programs, and services at individual, team, and organizational levels.
- The task of fostering mental health in a sport organization also is multi-disciplinary in nature and scope. Many contributors can play a part in enhancing and maintaining the positive mental health of athletes in sport organizations. Beyond qualified licensed health professionals, key contributors include coaches, staff, athletic administrators, athletes, and other stakeholders, such as family members.
- A commitment to program planning and evaluation will allow for experientially informed and evidence-based programs and services that address mental health needs of athletes. These programs and services in a sport organization can be developed and sustained, one at a time, in a progressive manner. This kind of program planning and evaluation approach involves needs assessment, program design, monitoring of program implementation, program evaluation, and the use of evaluation information for continuous development and improvement.
- An emphasis on continuous development and improvement of mental health programs and services highlights the value of developing a mentally healthy sport organization over the course of time. Given this commitment, the practitioner plays an important role: they make sure the programs address priority mental and emotional needs of athletes and others as the programs are designed and implemented.
- A practitioner must commit to the concept that fostering the mental health of athletes, coaches, and staff is embedded within relevant

social, ethnic, and cultural contexts of the sport organization. This contextual information is important and will determine in part how mental health programs are provided to athletes, coaches, and staff.

DEVELOPING A MENTALLY HEALTHY SPORT ORGANIZATION

Throughout the book, we have employed a systems approach to identify and act on a range of possibilities that can lead to the positive mental health of athletes, coaches, and staff. This book has covered a range of mental health-enhancing possibilities at individual, team, and organizational levels. Hopefully, you will be able to incorporate one or more of these possibilities into your work in building mentally healthy sport organizations.

As the book has pointed out, to develop a mentally healthy sport organization, you must not only clearly identify the organization, but you must also involve key contributors. In this regard, progress toward the development of a mentally healthy sport organization will be realized if you activate the following factors:

- *Availability of resources:* The sport organization makes available resources so it can promote mental health and provide mental health programs and services. These resources include qualified mental health providers, coaches, staff, and athletes; they also include clear purpose and goals, instructional methods, procedures, activities, facilities, and an operating budget.
- *Values are clarified:* The values of the sport organization affirm that the mental health of athletes, coaches, and staff is considered an important, integral aspect of the sport organization. As such, mental health is not marginalized as something to pay attention to only when an athlete has a problem.
- *Mental health is defined:* The nature and scope of what mental health means within the context of the sport organization has been defined and described. This recognition allows those involved in the operations of the organization (such as coaches and staff, as well as athletes) to understand the organization's definition of "mental health" and know how to contribute to mental health in positive, productive ways.
- *Leadership is present:* Leadership in the sport organization is present, willing, and able to take a public and programmatic stance to make certain mental health is a priority.

- *Time is managed:* The time to act in support of athletes, coaches, and staff mental health is at a premium; it needs to be managed in an effective and efficient way.
- *Obligation is evident:* Those individuals and groups who are part of the sport organization sense an obligation to ensure that no one stigmatizes the notion of mental health and that the mental health of athletes, coaches, and staff becomes a priority in the organization.
- *Resistance is addressed:* There is minimal resistance to mental health programs and services in the sport organization. When resistance occurs, leaders make concerted, transparent attempts to listen to and work with the individuals or parties toward a better understanding of mental health.
- *Yield is sought:* The yield or value of mental health can be seen through the proactive attempts to design, implement, and evaluate mental health programs and services. This process helps maintain and sustain the worthwhile features of the sport organization's mental health initiatives.

SYSTEMS APPROACH CHECKLIST

Throughout the book, a systems approach has served as the overarching framework for the task of fostering mental health in a sport organization, leading to a mentally healthy entity. As we conclude, I want to provide you with a systems approach checklist. I have formulated and used this checklist myself, successfully and productively, in all my mental health work in sport organizations. Furthermore, I find this checklist an important resource when I am checking my own work to ensure that it has addressed the basic tasks and activities covered in this book.

Although the book has covered in detail all the tasks and activities seen below, they are presented here in Table 14.1 in checklist format so you can use it as a basis for your work as a practitioner.

1. *Describe the sport organization:* You have clearly identified the sport organization within which you will promote and develop the mental health of athletes, coaches, and staff through programs and services.
2. *Identify mental health leadership:* You have identified the leaders who will guide and communicate the task of fostering the mental health of athletes, coaches, and staff in the sport organization.

Table 14.1 Systems Approach Checklist

Task	Not Yet	In Progress	Completed
Describe the sport organization			
Identify mental health leadership			
Commit to mental health			
Create a compelling vision			
Assess organizational readiness			
Involve key contributors			
Engage in mental health assessment			
Create valuable programs			
Educate about mental health			
Establish a team environment			
Develop the organizational level			
Coordinate across disciplines			
Value program evaluation			
Communicate and use information			
Adhere to ethical codes			

3. *Commit to mental health:* With the support and efforts of leadership, you have established their desire to develop a sport organization that can be a mentally healthy entity for athletes, coaches, and staff.

4. *Create a compelling vision:* Relevant stakeholders have discussed and agreed to a vision and multidisciplinary direction for fostering mental health.

5. *Assess organizational readiness:* An assessment has occurred concerning the readiness of the sport organization to engage in the task of fostering mental health in athletes, coaches, and staff.

6. *Involve key contributors:* Key contributors for the promotion and development of mental health in the sport organization have agreed to active involvement in the overall process. This includes qualified mental health professionals.

7. *Engage in mental health assessment:* Mental health assessment is viewed as an important part of learning about the mental health needs of athletes, coaches, and staff.

8. *Create valuable programs:* You have delineated a program planning and evaluation process that allows for the design, implementation,

and evaluation of mental health programs and services in the sport organization.

9. *Educate about mental health:* Coaches, staff, and other relevant stakeholders have been educated and trained about mental health and their own contributions to that area.

10. *Establish a team environment:* A team-level environment conducive to positive mental health has been established.

11. *Develop the organizational level:* Mental health policies, plans, and procedures have been formulated and enacted at the organizational level.

12. *Coordinate across disciplines:* You have utilized a multidisciplinary process so mental skills, life skills, and mental health can be coordinated at individual, team, and organizational levels.

13. *Value program evaluation:* A plan is in place and has been implemented for the evaluation of mental health programs as a basis for their continuous development and improvement.

14. *Communicate and use information:* Organizational stakeholders collaborate in the continuous development and improvement of mental health programs in the sport organizations.

15. *Adhere to ethical codes:* Mental health assessment and intervention occur according to ethical codes and legal strictures.

PROFESSIONAL PRACTICE DEVELOPMENT

Curiosity can be defined as a strong desire to know about or learn something. When an individual taps into their curiosity, they want to find out how things work and how they can make the things better (Brewer, 2021). Curiosity as a form of personal interest is enhanced when learning occurs (Blanchard et al., 2015).

Professional practice development in psychology and related mental health disciplines can benefit from the science of curiosity. When the practitioner's concern focuses on ensuring a sport organization is meeting the mental health needs of athletes, coaches, and staff, the practitioner—you or me—can leverage our curiosity. To be more specific, we can seek to become curious about mental health in sport organizations, asking what that area is and questioning how we can create and expand opportunities. We can inquire about issues such as the understanding of mental health in our setting. Likewise, we might question how we could employ a better and more context-specific way of assessing mental health needs or ask how we might make sure mental health is not marginalized. In these matters, we can take the lead to identify, formulate, and utilize frameworks, methods, and procedures to foster mental health in sport organizations.

I hope that the material covered in this book will pique your curiosity and propel you to take a leadership role regarding the mental health of athletes, coaches, and staff within sport organizations.

References

Abram, K. M., Paskar, L. D., Washburn, J. J., & Teplin, L. A. (2008). Perceived barriers to mental health services among youths in detention. *Journal of the American Academy of Child and Adolescent Psychiatry*, 47(3), 301–308. https://doi.org/10.1097/CHI.0b013e318160b3bb

Arnold, R., & Fletcher, D. (2012). A research synthesis and taxonomic classification of the organizational stressors encountered by sport performers. *Journal of Sport and Exercise Psychology*, 34(3), 397–429. https://doi.org/10.1123/jsep.34.3.397

Arnold, R. D., & Wade, J. P. (2015). A definition of systems thinking: A systems approach. *Procedia Computer Science*, 44, 669–678. https://doi.org/10.1016/j.procs.2015.03.050

Bauman, N. J. (2015). The stigma of mental health in athletes: Are mental toughness and mental health seen as contradictory in elite sport? *British Journal of Sports Medicine*, 50(3), 135–136. http://dx.doi.org/10.1136/bjsports-2015-095570

Blanchard, T. C., Hayden, B. Y., & Bromberg-Martin, E. S. (2015). Orbitofrontal cortex uses distinct codes for different choice attributes in decisions motivated by curiosity. *Neuron*, 85(3), 602–614. https://doi.org/10.1016/j.neuron.2014.12.050

Bisset, J. (2020). Supporting the psychological wellbeing of athletes: What can coaches do? *SIRCuit*. https://sirc.ca/blog/supporting-the-psychological-wellbeing-of-athletes-what-can-coaches-do/

Breslin, G., & Leavey, G. (2019). *Mental health and well-being interventions in sport: Research, theory, and practice*. Routledge. https://doi.org/10.4324/9781315147703

Breslin, G., Shannon, S., Haughey, T., Donnelly, P., & Leavey, G. (2017). A systematic review of interventions to increase awareness of mental health and well-being in athletes, coaches and officials. *Systematic Reviews*, 6, 177. https://doi.org/10.1186/s13643-017-0568-6

Brewer, B. W., & Redmond, C. J. (2017). *The psychology of sport injury*. Human Kinetics.

Brewer, J. (2021). *Unwinding anxiety: New science shows how to break the cycles of worry and fear to heal your mind*. Avery Penguin Random House.

Brown, G. T. (Ed.). (2014). *Mind, body and sport: Understanding and supporting student-athlete mental wellness*. National Collegiate Athletic Association. https://www.ncaapublications.com/p-4375-mind-body-and-sport-understanding-and-supporting-student-athlete-mental-wellness.aspx

Côté, J., & Gilbert, W. (2009). An integrative definition of coaching effectiveness and expertise. *International Journal of Sports Science & Coaching,* 4(3), 307–323. https://doi.org/10.1260/174795409789623892

Cruickshank, A., & Collins, D. (2012). Culture change in elite sport performance teams: Examining and advancing effectiveness in the new era. *Journal of Applied Sport Psychology,* 24(3), 338–355. https://doi.org/10.1080/10413200.2011.650819

Cunningham, G. B. (2011). *Diversity in sport organizations* (2nd ed.). Holcomb Hathaway.

Damschroder, L. J., Aron, D. C., Keith, R. E., Kirsch, S. R., Alexander, J. A., & Lowery, J. C. (2009). Fostering implementation of health services research findings into practice: A consolidated framework for advancing implementation science. *Implementation Science,* 4, 50–61. https://doi.org/10.1186/1748-5908-4-50

Dominici, G. (2012). Why does systems thinking matter? *Business Systems Review,* 1(1), 1–2. https://ssrn.com/abstract=2046736

Dweck, C. S. (2016). *Mindset: The new psychology of success.* Ballantine Books.

Duffy, J., Rooney, B., & Matthews, J. (2019). Coaches' mental health literacy and role perceptions for supporting young people's mental health. *Journal of Applied Sport Psychology,* 33(1), 45–59. https://doi.org/10.1080/10413200.2019.1646840

Fletcher, D., & Arnold, R. (2017). Stress in sport: The role of the organizational environment. In C. R. D. Wagstaff (Ed.), *Organizational psychology in sport: Key issues and practical applications* (pp. 83–100). Routledge. https://doi.org/10.4324/9781315666532

Fletcher, D., & Sarkar, M. (2012). A grounded theory of psychological resilience in Olympic champions. *Psychology of Sport and Exercise,* 13(5), 669–678. https://doi.org/10.1016/j.psychsport.2012.04.007

Fletcher, T. B., Benshoff, J. M., & Richburg, M. J. (2003). A systems approach to understanding and counseling college student-athletes. *Journal of College Counseling,* 6, 35–45. https://doi.org/10.1002/j.2161-1882.2003.tb00225.x

Flett, M. R., Sackett, S. C., & Camiré, M. (2017). Understanding effective coaching: Antecedents and consequences. In R. Thelwell, C. Harwood, & I. Greenlees (Eds.), *The psychology of sports coaching: Research and practice.* Routledge. https://doi.org/10.4324/9781315689210

Fogaca, J. L. (2021). Combining mental health and performance interventions: Coping and social support for student-athletes. *Journal of Applied Sport Psychology,* 33(1), 4–19. https://doi.org/10.1080/10413200.2019.1648326

Galderisi, S., Heinz, A., Kastrup, M., Beezhold, J., & Sartorius, N. (2015). Toward a new definition of mental health. *World Psychiatry,* 14(2), 231–233. https://doi.org/10.1002/wps.20231

Galli, N., & Gonzalez, S. P. (2014). Psychological resilience in sport: A review of the literature and implications for research and practice. *International Journal of Sport and Exercise Psychology,* 13(3), 243–257. https://doi.org/10.1080/1612197X.2014.946947

Gardner, F. L., & Moore, Z. E. (2007). *The psychology of enhancing human performance: The mindfulness-acceptance-commitment (MAC) approach.* Springer. https://doi.org/10.1891/9780826103369

Gavrilova, Y., & Donohue, B. (2018). Sport-specific mental health interventions in athletes: A call for optimization models sensitive to sport culture. *Journal of Sport Behavior*, 41(3), 288–304.

Gilmore, S. (2017). Attitudes to employ in sport organizations. In C. R. D. Wagstaff (Ed.), *Organizational psychology in sport: Key issues and practical applications* (pp. 62–80). Routledge. https://doi.org/10.4324/9781315666532.

Gonzalez, J. M., Alegria, M., & Prihoda, T. J. (2005). How do attitudes toward mental health treatment vary by age, gender, and ethnicity/race in young adults? *Journal of Community Psychology*, 33(5), 611–629. https://doi.org/10.1002/jcop.20071

Gouttebarge, V., Bindra, A., Blauwet, C., Campriani, N., Currie, A., Engebretson, L., Hainline, B., Kroshus, E., McDuff, D., Mountjoy, M. L., Purcell, R., Putukian, M., Reardon, C. L., Rice, S. M., & Budgett, R. (2020). International Olympic Committee (IOC) sport mental health assessment tool 1 (SMAHT-1) and sport mental health recognition tool 1 (SMHRT-1): Towards better support of athletes' mental health. *British Journal of Sports Medicine*, 55(1), 30–37. http://dx.doi.org/10.1136/bjsports-2020-102411

Gouttebarge, V., Castaldelli-Maia, J. M., Gorczynski, P., Hainline, B., Hitchcock, M. E., Kerkhoffs, G. M., Rice, S. M., & Reardon, C. L. (2019). Occurrence of mental health symptoms and disorders in current and former elite athletes: A systematic review and meta-analysis. *British Journal of Sports Medicine*, 53(11), 700–706. https://doi.org/10.1136/bjsports-2019-100671

Halberstam, D. (2005). *The education of a coach*. Hachette.

Haugen, E. N. J., Thome, J., Pietrucha, M. E., & Levin, M. P. (2018). Mental health screening: Identifying clinical issues. In J. Taylor (Ed.), *Assessment in applied sport psychology* (pp. 59–72). Human Kinetics.

Haver, A., Akerjordet, K., Caputi, P., Furunes, T., & Magee, C. (2015). Measuring mental well-being: A validation of the short Warwick-Edinburgh mental well-being scale in Norwegian and Swedish. *Scandinavian Journal of Public Health*, 43(7), 721–727. https://doi.org/10.1177/1403494815588862

Hegarty, J., & Huelsmann, C. (2020). *ACT in sport: Improve performance through mindfulness, acceptance, and commitment*. Dark River Press.

Henriksen, K., Schinke, R., McCann, S., Durand-Bush, N., Moesch, K., Parham, W. D., Larsen, C. H., Cogan, K., Donaldson, A., Poczwardowski, A., Noce, F., & Hunziker, J. (2020). Athlete mental health in the Olympic/Paralympic quadrennium: A multi-societal consensus statement. *International Journal of Sport and Exercise Psychology*, 18(3), 391–408. https://doi.org/10.1080/1612197X.2020.1746379

Henriksen, K., Schinke, R., Moesch, K., McCann, S., Parham, W. D., Larsen, C. H., & Terry, P. (2019). Consensus statement on improving the mental health of high performance athletes. *International Journal of Sport and Exercise Psychology*, 18(5), 553–560. https://doi.org/10.1080/1612197X.2019.1570473

Hong, E., & Rao, A. L. (2020). *Mental health in the athlete: Modern perspectives and novel challenges for the sports medicine provider*. Springer. https://doi.org/10.1007/978-3-030-44754-0

Kaufmann, K. A., Glass, C. R., & Pineau, T. R. (2018). *Mindful sport performance enhancement: Mental training for athletes and coaches*. American Psychological Association.

Kessler, R. C., Berglund, P., Demler, O., Jin, R., Merikangas, K. R., & Walters, E. E. (2005). Lifetime prevalence and age-of-onset distributions of DSM-IV disorders in the National Comorbidity Survey Replication. *Archives in General Psychiatry*, 62(6), 593–602. https://doi.org/10.1001/archpsyc.62.6.593

Keyes, C. L. M. (2002). The mental health continuum: From languishing to flourishing in life. *Journal of Health and Social Behavior*, 43(2), 207–222. https://doi.org/10.2307/3090197

Keyes, C. L. M. (2007). Promoting and protecting mental health as flourishing: A complementary strategy for improving rational mental health. *American Psychologist*, 62(2), 95–108. https://doi.org/10.1037/0003-066X.62.2.95

Keyes, C. L. M. (2013). Promoting and protecting positive mental health: Early and often throughout the lifespan. In C. L. M. Keyes (Ed.), *Mental well-being: International contributions to the study of positive mental health* (pp. 3–28). Springer.

Lee, A. N., & Taylor, J. (2018). Science of sport psychology assessment. In J. Taylor (Ed.), *Assessment in applied sport psychology* (pp. 15–24). Human Kinetics.

Li, J., Li, J., Huang, Y., & Thornicroft, G. (2014). Mental health training program for community mental health staff in Guangzhou, China: Effects on knowledge of mental illness and stigma. *International Journal of Mental Health Systems*, 8(49), 1–6. https://doi.org/10.1186/1752-4458-8-49

Liddle, S. K., Deane, F. P., Batterham, M., & Vella, S. (2021). A brief sports-based mental health literacy program for male adolescents: A cluster-randomized controlled trial. *Journal of Applied Sport Psychology*, 33(1), 20–44. https://doi.org/10.1080/10413200.2019.1653404

Lingard, L., Espin, S., Rubin, B., Whyte, S., Colmenares, M., Baker, G. R., Doran, D., Grober, E., Orser, B., Bohnen, J., & Reznick, R. (2005). Getting teams to talk: Development and pilot implementation of a checklist to promote interprofessional communication in the OR. *Quality and Safety in Health Care*, 14(5), 340–346. http://dx.doi.org/10.1136/qshc.2004.012377

MacIntrye, T., Jones, M., Brewer, B. W., Van Raalte, J., O'Shea, D., & McCarthy, P. J. (2017). Editorial: Mental health challenges in elite sport: Balancing risk with reward. *Frontiers in Psychology*, 8, 1892. https://doi.org/10.3389/fpsyg.2017.01892

Maher, C. A. (2011). *The complete mental game of baseball: Taking charge of the process, on and off the field*. Authorhouse.

Maher, C. A. (2012). *Planning and evaluating human services programs: A resource guide for practitioners*. Authorhouse.

Maher, C. A. (2017). Working within professional baseball: Reflections and recommendations on the practice of sport and performance psychology. In R. J. Schinke & D. Hackfort (Eds.), *Psychology in professional sports and the performing arts: Challenges and strategies* (pp. 229–240). Routledge. https://doi.org/10.4324/9781315750569

Maher, C. A. (2021a). *Developing and sustaining sport psychology programs: A resource guide for practitioners*. Routledge. https://doi.org/10.4324/9780429326523

Maher, C. A. (2021b). Enhancing the mental performance of head coaches in professional sports: A case study of collaboration with the head coach of a professional basketball team. *Case Studies in Sport and Exercise Psychology*, 5(1), 61–68. https://doi.org/10.1123/cssep.2020-0031

Maher, C. A., & Taylor, J. (2018). Systems approach to consulting in sport organizations. In J. Taylor (Ed.), *Assessment in applied sport psychology* (pp. 235–244). Human Kinetics.

Maher, C. A., & Taylor, J. (2020a). Long term. In J. Taylor (Ed.), *Comprehensive applied sport psychology* (pp. 37–42). Routledge. https://doi.org/10.4324/9780429503689

Maher, C. A., & Taylor, J. (2020b). Team management. In J. Taylor (Ed.), *Comprehensive applied sport psychology* (pp. 380–385). Routledge. https://doi.org/10.4324/9780429503689

McGraw, S. A., Deubert, C. R., Lynch, H. F., Nozzolillo, A., Taylor, L., & Cohen, I. G. (2018). Life on an emotional roller coaster: NFL players and their family members' perspectives on player mental health. *Journal of Clinical Sport Psychology*, 12(3), 404–431. https://doi.org/10.1123/jcsp.2017-0051

Meadows, D. H. (2008). *Thinking in systems: A primer*. Chelsea Green Publishing.

Moesch, K., Kenttä, G., Kleinert, J., Quignon-Fleuret, C., Cecil, S., & Bertello, M. (2018). FEPSAC position statement: Mental health disorders in elite athletes and models of service provision. *Psychology of Sport and Exercise*, 38, 61–71. https://doi.org/10.1016/j.psychsport.2018.05.013

Moore, Z. (2009). Theoretical and empirical developments of the mindfulness-acceptance-commitment approach (MAC) to performance enhancement. *Journal of Clinical Sport Psychology*, 3(4), 291–302. https://doi.org/10.1123/jcsp.3.4.291

Moreland, J. J., Coxe, K. A., & Yang, J. (2018). Collegiate athletes' mental health services utilization: A systematic review of conceptualizations, operationalizations, facilitators, and barriers. *Journal of Sport and Health Science*, 7(1), 58–69. https://doi.org/10.1016/j.jshs.2017.04.009

Morgeson, F. P. (2005). The external leadership of self-managing teams: Intervening in the context of novel and disruptive events. *Journal of Applied Psychology*, 90(3), 497–508. https://doi.org/10.1037/0021-9010.90.3.497

Muir, I. L., & Munroe-Chandler, K. J. (2020). Using infographics to promote athletes' mental health: Recommendations for sport psychology consultants. *Journal of Sport Psychology in Action*, 11(3), 143–164. https://doi.org/10.1080/21520704.2020.1738607

National Council for Behavioral Health (2015). *Mental health first aid USA*. National Council for Behavioral Health.

Neal, T. L., Diamond, A. B., Goldman, S., Klossner, D., Morse, E. D., Pajak, D. E., Putukian, M., Quandt, E. F., Sullivan, J. P., Wallack, C., & Welzant, V. (2013). Inter-association recommendations for developing a plan to recognize and refer student-athletes with psychological concerns at the collegiate level: An executive summary of a consensus statement. *Journal of Athletic Training*, 48(5), 716–720. https://doi.org/10.4085/1062-6050-48.4.13

Neil, R., MacFarlane, H. M., & Smith, A. P. (2017). Well-being in sport organizations. In C. R. D. Wagstaff (Ed.), *Organizational psychology in sport: Key issues and practical applications* (pp. 101–119). Routledge. https://doi.org/10.4324/9781315666532

Paquette, K., & Trudel, P. (2018). Learner-centered coach education: Practical recommendations for coach development administrators. *International Sport Coaching Journal*, 5(2), 169–175. https://doi.org/10.1123/iscj.2017-0084

Poucher, Z. A., Tamminen, K. A., Kerr, G., & Cairney, J. (2021). A commentary on mental health research in elite sport. *Journal of Applied Sport Psychology*, 33(1), 60–82. https://doi.org/10.1080/10413200.2019.1668496

Raabe, J., & Zakrajsek, R. A. (2017). Coaches and teammates as social agents for collegiate athletes' basic psychological need satisfaction. *Journal of Intercollegiate Sport*, 10(1), 67–82. https://doi.org/10.1123/jis.2016-0033

Reardon, C. L., & Factor, R. M. (2010). Sport psychiatry: A systematic review of diagnosis and medical treatment of mental illness in athletes. *Sports Medicine*, 40(11), 961–980. https://doi.org/10.2165/11536580-000000000-00000

Reardon, C. L., Hainline, B., Aron, C. M., Baron, D., Baum, A. L., Bindra, A., Budgett, R., Campriani, N., Castaldelli-Maia, J. M., Currie, A., Derevensky, J. L., Glick, I. D., Gorczynski, P., Gouttebarge, V., Grandner, M. A., Han, D. H., McDuff, D., Mountjoy, M., Polat, A., ... & Engebretsen, L. (2019). Mental health in elite athletes: International Olympic Committee consensus statement. *British Journal of Sports Medicine*, 53, 667–699. http://dx.doi.org/10.1136/bjsports-2019-100715

Rice, S. M., Parker, A. G., Mawren, D., Clifton, P., Harcourt, P., Lloyd, M., Kountouris, A., Smith, B., McGorry, P. D., & Purcell, R. (2019). Preliminary psychometric validation of a brief screening tool for athlete mental health among male elite athletes: The Athlete Psychological Strain Questionnaire. *International Journal of Sport and Exercise Psychology*, 18(6), 850–865. https://doi.org/10.1080/1612197X.2019.1611900

Rice, S. M., Purcell, R., DeSilva, S., Mawren, D., McGorry, P. D., & Parker, A. G. (2016). The mental health of elite athletes: A narrative systematic review. *Sports Medicine*, 46(9), 1333–1353. https://doi.org/10.1007/s40279-016-0492-2

Schinke, R., Papaioannou, A., Maher, C., Parham, W. D., Larsen, C. H., Gordin, R., & Cotterill, S. (2020). Sport psychology services to professional athletes: Working though COVID-19. *International Journal of Sport and Exercise Psychology*, 18(4), 1–5. https://doi.org/10.1080/1612197X.2020.1766182

Schinke, R. J., Stambulova, N. B., Si, G., & Moore, Z. (2018). International society of sport psychology position stand: Athletes' mental health, performance, and development. *International Journal of Sport and Exercise Psychology*, 16(6), 622–639. https://doi.org/10.1080/1612197X.2017.1295557

Sebbens, J., Hassmén, P., Crisp, D., & Wensley, K. (2016). Mental health in sport (MHS): Improving the early intervention knowledge and confidence of elite sport staff. *Frontiers in Psychology*, 7, 911. https://doi.org/10.3389/fpsyg.2016.00911

Shannon, S., Hanna, D., Haughey, T., Leavey, G., McGeown, C., & Breslin, G. (2019). Effects of a mental health intervention in athletes: Applying self-determination theory. *Frontiers in Psychology*, 10, 1875. https://doi.org/10.3389/fpsyg.2019.01875

Shim, R. S., Baltrus, P., Ye, J., & Rust, G. (2011). Prevalence, treatment, and control of depression symptoms in the United States. *The Journal of the American Board of Family Medicine*, 24(1), 33–38. https://doi.org/10.3122/jabfm.2011.01.100121

Simmons, L., Jones, T., & Bradley, E. (2017). Reducing mental health stigma: The relationship between knowledge and attitude change. *European Journal of Mental Health*, 12(1), 25–40. https://doi.org/10.5708/EJMH.12.2017.1.2

Taylor, J. (2018). Importance of assessment in sport psychology consulting. In J. Taylor (Ed.), *Assessment in applied sport psychology* (pp. 3–14). Human Kinetics.

Thelwell, R. C., Grenlees, I. A., & Weston, N. J. V. (2006). Using psychological skills training to develop soccer performance. *Journal of Applied Sport Psychology*, 18(3), 254–270. https://doi.org/10.1080/10413200600830323

Tomalski, J., Clevinger, K., Albert, E., Jackson, R., Wartalowicz, K., & Petrie, T. A. (2019). Mental health screening for athletes: Program development, implementation, and evaluation. *Journal of Sport Psychology in Action*, 10(2), 121–135. https://doi.org/10.1080/21520704.2019.1604589

Van Raalte, J. L., Cornelius, A. E., Andrews, S., Diehl, N. S., & Brewer, B. W. (2015). Mental health referral for student-athletes: Web-based education and training. *Journal of Clinical Sport Psychology*, 9(3), 197–212. https://doi.org/10.1123/jcsp.2015-0011

Vella, S. A., Swann, C., & Tamminen, K. A. (2021). Mental health in sport: An overview and introduction to the special issue. *Journal of Applied Sport Psychology*, 33(1), 1–3. https://doi.org/10.1080/10413200.2020.1854897

Wagstaff, C. R. D., (2017). Organizational psychology in sport: An introduction. In C. R. D. Wagstaff (Ed.), *Organizational psychology in sport: Key issues and practical applications* (pp. 1–7). Routledge. https://doi.org/10.4324/9781315666532

Walsh, R. (2011). Lifestyle and mental health. *American Psychologist*, 66(7), 579–592. https://doi.org/10.1037/a0021769

World Health Organization. (2004). *Promoting mental health: Concepts, emerging evidence, practice (summary report)*. World Health Organization. https://apps.who.int/iris/handle/10665/42940

World Health Organization. (2013). *Mental health action plan (2013–2020)*. https://www.who.int/publications/i/item/9789241506021

PURPOSE

As members of our organization, we interact with players and staff on a regular basis. At times, we may encounter players, coaches, or staff whose behavior causes concern, or players may express their own concern for managing their overall well-being. The purpose of this crisis and emergency action plan is to provide members of our organization with the following resources: (1) definition of mental health; (2) descriptions of challenging mental health situations that may occur in our organizational environment; and (3) roles and responsibilities of persons who can facilitate mental health response.

DEFINITION OF MENTAL HEALTH

Mental health reflects your psychological, emotional, and social functioning as a person, over and above your work. You can take responsibility for developing and maintaining positive mental health by managing how you use your thoughts, emotions, and actions.

MENTAL HEALTH PROBLEM, CRISIS, AND EMERGENCY ACTION SITUATIONS

Mental health situations that require interventions and responses can include a range of situations:

- *Mental health problem:* This is a situation where a player, coach, or staff member believes they have a problem that is directly affecting their mental health, including possibly on the field performance. In this kind of situation, the individual seems motivated to discuss the problem with a mental health professional.
- *Mental health referral:* This kind of situation evolves out of a mental health problem situation. Here, the player, coach, or staff member

agrees to a referral to a licensed mental health professional associated with our organization.

- *Mental health crisis:* This is a situation that is non-life threatening. However, the player, coach, or staff member is in a very problematic situation (crisis). Thus, the individual requires immediate mental health care, most likely within a 24-hour time period. The kind of care provided may include out-patient assistance, partial hospitalization, or in-patient treatment.
- *Mental health emergency:* This situation is life-threatening and requires rapid and immediate attention, and it may very well require hospitalization.

MENTAL HEALTH ROLES AND RESPONSIBILITIES

While we are part of the solution for positive mental health within our organization, there are key professional resources throughout the organization available to facilitate mental health plans related to problem, crisis, and emergency situations. The professional resources with each team and at each site are as follows:

- *Licensed mental health professional:* Responsible for overseeing responses of organizational employees to challenging mental health situations.
- *Mental performance coaches:* Responsible for listening to players, coaches, and staff about their mental health needs and concerns and then encouraging them to reach out for professional assistance (including to the mental health team).
- *Athletic trainers and strength coaches:* Same responsibilities as mental performance coaches.
- *Mental health leadership team:* Responsible for making sure players, coaches, and staff receive appropriate mental health care.

NOTE
1 For the sake of confidentiality, names and specific responsibilities have been omitted.

TITLE AND RELEVANT CONTEXT OF THE MENTAL HEALTH PROGRAM

The title of the mental health program is *Player Personal Development Program*. This program is best considered a preventive mental health program. It is part of a series of sport psychology programs designed to assist Major League Baseball players to grow and develop mentally and emotionally.

OVERVIEW OF THE PROGRAM'S PARTICIPANTS

Participants are 25 players of a major league professional baseball team. These players include pitchers and position players. A total of 10 of the players have five or more years of playing baseball at the major league level; 12 of the players have less than three years of major league service. Of the 25 players, 11 are from a Latin American country. All players speak English.

PURPOSE AND GOALS OF THE PROGRAM

The purpose of the program is to enable major league players, as program participants, to learn how they can balance playing baseball with the rest of their lives.

The goals of the program are:

1. Learn to clarify their values as a person, over and above playing baseball.
2. Learn how to identify their personal strong points and areas in need of development.
3. Learn how to cope in an effective way with people, places, and things that can derail them as well as those that can support their growth and development.

PROGRAM ORGANIZATION

The content of this program is organized by several separate yet interrelated group meetings with the players in addition to individual one-on-one meetings. The program is voluntary in that a player does not have to attend the program, if they so desire.

The group meetings occur for one hour a week over the course of spring training and the baseball season. Each scheduled meeting involves group discussion about the topic and activities that involve the participants. The topics of these weekly meetings include the following examples:

- Understanding values and why are they important to me and others.
- Taking steps to clarify and keep in contact with my values.
- Anchoring my work and decisions to my values.
- Assessing my strong points and limitations as a person.
- Coping effectively with people, places, and things that I encounter.

The individual sessions occur throughout the program with one of the program staff, at the request of the player.

PROGRAM PERSONNEL

The program was conducted by the director of sport psychology for the organization who is a licensed psychologist. Two of the sport organization's mental performance coaches assisted the director.

Index

Note: Page references in *italics* denote figures, and in **bold** tables.

life skills 11, 142; mental health
    programs and services 137–139;
    nature of 137–139; scope of
    137–139
Love, Kevin 3

Major League Baseball 2
mental and emotional development
    coping skills program 83
mental and emotional outcomes
    11–12, **12**
mental and emotional strengths 84–85;
    benefits of 68–69; goals of 67;
    levels of 69–74, 70; and needs
    assessment 62–63, 66–69
mental development 10–11; assessment
    of 59–61
mental health 142; benefits of vision
    about 27–28; circumstances
    pertaining to 43–44; clinical
    evaluation 63; communicating
    with athletes 11, 110;
    conceptions, related to sport
    4; concern 106, **107**; creating
    team environment 114–115;
    crisis 107, **107**, 131–132,
    185; defined of 184; domain
    139–140; emergency 107, **107**,
    185; evolution, related to sport
    1–3; idea of 42–43; inquiry 106,
    107; leadership team 185; as
    multidisciplinary responsibility
    48–50; nature of 117–118; and
    obligation 44–45; policies about
    importance of 125–128; positive
    expectations 119–120; problem
    106, **107**, 184–185; rationale for
    a vision about 26–27; reinforce
    talk about 118–119; and resistance
    45; roles and responsibilities 185;
    scope of 117–118; situations and
    responsibilities 106–107, **107**;
    and timing 44; viewpoints of team
    members 118; and yield 45–46

mental health assessment: defined 129;
    policy about 129–130; *see also*
    assessment of mental/emotional
    development of athletes
mental health clinicians: relationships
    53; requirements 53;
    responsibilities 53; role 53
mental health committee: members 31;
    and mental health vision statement
    30–31; responsibilities of 31
mental health contributors 50–51;
    educating coaches and staff as
    100–113; education and training
    programs for 111–112; 4Rs
    framework 50, 50–51; meetings
    56–57; relationships of 51;
    requirements of 51; roles and
    responsibilities as 50–51, 109;
    securing commitment of 55–56, 56;
    supervision of 57; training coaches
    and staff as 100–113; types 51–55
mental health first aid 102
mental health initiatives: assessing
    readiness of sport organization for
    33–47; defined 27, 33–35
mental health in sport organizations:
    defined 5–7; positive 5–6; risk and
    protective factors 7–10; systems
    approach to 17–25
mental health literacy 83, 102
mental health plans 124; areas for
    formulation and enactment of
    124–132; nature and scope of 124;
    rationale for 122–124
mental health policies 107–108,
    124; areas for formulation and
    enactment of 124–132; nature
    and scope of 124; rationale for
    122–124
mental health procedures 107–108,
    124; areas for formulation and
    enactment of 124–132; nature
    and scope of 124; rationale for
    122–124

mental health professionals: collaborating with 111; policy about qualified 128–129; *see also* licensed mental health professionals; mental health clinicians

mental health program evaluation 93–94; communication 160; conducting 150–151; deciding on 153; defined 151–152; describing design of 155; establishing team 152–153; formulating plan 154–158; identifying program evaluation staff 158; implementing plan 158–159; information 160; participation in 149–150; plan 154–159; program evaluation question 155–156; report, constructing 159; selecting data collection methods 156–158; selecting procedures to answer the questions 156–158; specifying purpose of 154–155; steps to conduct 150, 150–160

mental health programs: action plan 168, **169**; clarifying need for 142; continuous development and improvement of 162–163; coordination 133–135, 144; coordination procedural guidelines 141–144; and decision-makers 164–165; decision making 161–162, 167–168; defined 82, 143, 147; delineate supervisory roles 143–144; design of 165–166; evaluable program design for 186–187; evaluation 93–94, 145–147; evaluation report 159; evaluation team 152–153; examples of 82–84; formulating evaluable design of 90–92; framework for developing 163–169, **169**; identifying 164–165; identifying providers

143; implementation 92; life skills domain 137–139; mental health domain 139–140; mental skills domain 135–137; nature and scope of 147–149; organization 187; participants 186; participation in evaluation of 149–150; personnel 187; purpose and goals of 89–90, 186; resources 82; review program evaluation 166–167; supervision and related matters 140–141; title and relevant context of 186; typology of 94–99; utilization of resources in 147–148, **148**

mental health programs development process 79–81, 81; mental/emotional needs assessment of participants 87, **88**; nature of 85–94; participants of program 86–87, **87**; scope of 85–94

mental health referral 63, 85, 95–96, 106, **107**, 184–185; defined 130; design of 96; mental health needs 96; policy about 130; purpose of 76–77, 96; target population for 96

mental health screening 63, 74–76, 95; design of 95; instruments 75; mental health needs 95; purpose of 95; target population for 95

mental health services: clarifying need for 142; defined 82; delineate supervisory roles 143–144; describing 143; evaluating coordination 144; examples of 84–85; identifying providers 143; typology of 94–99

mental health vision statement 27–28; communication 31–32; drafting 28–30, 29; and mental health committee 30–31; nature of 28–31; scope of 28–31

mentally healthy sport organization: and assessment of mental/emotional